THE SCILLY ISLES

In Tresco Gardens

THE SCILLY ISLES

GEOFFREY GRIGSON

with illustrations by
Fred Uhlman

DUCKWORTH

Lighthouse of St. Agnes

CONTENTS

1. THE SCENE AND THE COLOUR .... page 7
2. ISLAND HISTORY AND PREHISTORY 10
3. THE SCILLONIANS 16
4. TRESCO AND NORTHWETHEL 18
5. ST. HELEN'S 24
6. TEAN 26
7. KELPING 29
8. SAMSON 30
9. BRYHER 33
10. ST. MARTIN'S AND WHITE ISLAND 39
11. THE EASTERN ISLANDS 44
12. ST. AGNES AND THE GUGH 46
13. ANNET 50
14. ROSEVEAR 51
15. WRECKS 53
16. MINCARLO, IN THE NORTHERN ROCKS 56
17. ST. MARY'S 57
    BIBLIOGRAPHY 59

NOTE

ANYONE WHO WRITES even the shortest book on the Isles of Scilly must draw from the observers who have been there before him: Heath, Borlase, Troutbeck, Woodley—especially Woodley—and be grateful for their record of a community which was changing quickly even in their time. I have plundered many more books (in particular H. O'Neill Hencken's *Archaeology of Cornwall and Scilly*), and many pamphlets and articles, most of which are listed in the belief that these very peculiar scraps of England will make those who visit them once, visit them twice and three times and compel them to be inquisitive about details of every kind. The miniature universe of Scilly needs describing in more than its shape and colour. In one's feeling for the islands, sea and sky and land are all mixed with inhabitants, living and dead, human and non-human, animal and vegetable, and with Scilly's ancient remains.

I owe many thanks—too many for so small a return. But I must name J. E. Lousley, who lent me published and unpublished papers on Scillonian plants; J. E. Gover who let me see and use his unpublished notes on the place-names of Scilly; Dr. Glyn Daniel, who has saved me from some archaeological blundering; Professor E. G. Bowen; and not least, several islanders, Major A. A. Dorrien-Smith of Tresco, Vernon Thompson of St. Mary's, and friends, especially, on St. Martin's: Sidney Bond, Laddie Goddard, Bernard Bond, Wilfred Christopher, and the Rev. H. A. Lewis.

Since I wrote this small book in 1948, as an introduction, with my friend Fred Uhlman's illustrations, to the islands in light, colour, physique and history, archaeologists have been dragging ancient Scilly out of the dark. So I have made corrections and additions. Also I have brought the bibliography up to date, helped in this with information kindly supplied by Charles Thomas, of the Institute of Cornish Studies, who has conducted important excavations in Scilly, and is now working on an account of Scillonian place-names.

Broad Town, 1976   G. E. G.

This revised re-set edition first published in 1977 by
GERALD DUCKWORTH & CO LTD
The Old Piano Factory,
43 Gloucester Crescent, London NW1

Original edition published in 1948

Text © 1977 Geoffrey Grigson
Illustrations copyright Gerald Duckworth & Co Ltd

All rights reserved. No part of this publication may be reproduced, stored in a retrieval system, or transmitted, in any form or by any means, electronic, mechanical, photocopying, recording or otherwise, without the prior permission of the publisher.

Cloth ISBN 0 7156 1103 8
Paper ISBN 0 7156 1104 6

Printed in Gt Britain by
Page Bros (Norwich) Ltd
Mile Cross Lane
Norwich

1
THE SCENE AND THE COLOUR

LEFT TO THEMSELVES the multitudinous Isles of Scilly would no doubt be what many of the small, ungrazed, untilled, uninhabited islands are today: they would be knolls of granite rising out of a dense scrub of bracken, coarse grass, honeysuckle and inhuman brambles. They would be, in fact, what their Governor, and Lord Proprietor, Francis Godolphin, declared they had been in the sixteenth century, a "bushment of briars"—if not, as he went on, a refuge for pirates. The Atlantic would cover and uncover the beaches of clear, clean sand. But like rodents, human beings creep ashore upon most of the islands of the seas of the world on which life and cultivation are possible; and for some four thousand years, at least, the Isles of Scilly have not been left to themselves. Their landscape and their vegetation have been modified, granite tombs have been left behind on the high points, trees have been planted, churches and villages have been built, farms laid out and enclosed, harbours have been shaped, lighthouses and landmarks have been erected.

Yet the first attraction of the islands is to be found both in this modification and in its limits. Southerly as they are for us, the islands are northern and barbarian and rough, rather than tropical and fecund. They are small islands, slight rafts or platforms surrounded by an immensity of sea and arched by an even greater immensity of sky. No doubt they have never been so well cultivated, no doubt their inhabitants have never been so prosperous; but if you throw your eye around the islands from the high point of Bryher, or from the ramparts of Star Castle, in the metropolitan island of St. Mary's, above the capital of Hugh Town (which is the seat of government and the centre of commerce and shipping), you realise how little the modification is, to how small a degree the roughness of the islands has been humanised. The winds keep the houses low; the isolation, the distance (which is 27 miles) from the mainland have insisted that the materials should be local. So the older houses, as well as low, are grey—grey granite, with grey-groated roofs. On Tresco, there are dark plantations of Californian pine. Yet seen across the central lagoon of the islands, the plantations look small, as indeed they are, in relation to the mass of Tresco. If, from one of these high places you are surveying the islands in September, the dominant colour upon them, sweeping up and round the low hills, is the wet rust of bracken. It is the colour of uncultivated parts, of that majority of the land surface which never can be used. Moreover, only St. Mary's, Agnes, Bryher, Tresco, and St. Martin's (unless one includes the lighthouse crag of Round Island) are inhabited and cultivated in their small acres and nooks and corners.

Your inclusive, autumnal view takes in all the desert islands, all the compact group of the Eastern Islands—all the islands which are so little described in the books and the guidebooks, and which are so much in the scene, and the source of so much in one's reactions to the shape, the colours, and the circuit of the group. The islands are raw and original in the whole, humanised only in the detail. The detail is rich, curious, coloured, varied and variegated. The whole and the detail, inhuman and human, big and very small, weave into each other movingly, as one comes to the exploration of the islands. But it is the original which governs, the human which is incidental. A small bulb field will be hedged with purple flowering veronica from New Zealand, but the nature of the islands, the high winds off the Atlantic, will have bent the veronicas into shape, and the humidity will have muffled the gnarled, prematurely old branches with rough lichens beneath the improbable leaves and flowers. An old boot lies on a shingle bar: it will be a golden boot, golden again with lichen. Above the beach, at Higher Town on St. Martin's, stretch, side by side, some long, low boat-houses. Wind-driven moisture off the sea has burned their galvanised roofs to the brightness of dead bracken. In the graveyards, the tombstones are pushed over this way and that, drunkenly, among wiry mats of long grass and brambles. Throughout the islands, in fact, the original continually fends against the human incident. There is a continual struggle in which one form of life tries to bring death to another form of life, and all its products. The sea at the far end of St. Martin's, facing Tean, drives in against a field, which shows a clean-cut, retreating face towards Tean Sound. Sticking out of the face are bits and pieces of older living on the islands, stems of clay pipes, rims of earthenware bowls, brown and yellow sherds of seventeenth-century slip-ware.

In the past, wrecks, year in, year out, spoke of the immense power of the raw and the original, the immense impact of wind and water upon granite. Navigational aids make the Scillies less fearful. The recurrent white eye from the Bishop Lighthouse and the red eye from the lighthouse on Round Island are reminders of this reduced fear, the tombstones in the churchyards show agonisingly what this fear has meant; but it was always a fear, in the main, from outside. It has, and had, less to do with the internal tensions and struggles of the group, the internal, the *island*, struggle between the whole and the human; which has gone on for several thousand years, and still goes on. Wrecks were agonising to the wrecked, but wreckage and wrecked cargoes have often been a blessing. The wind drops, the clouds clear away, the central sea between the islands deepens in its colour; one feels an immense calm and felicity and cleanliness. If the wind rises, and the sea with it, or fog creeps up and round, the calm dissolves in uneasiness, smallness, and isolation. The boat from Penzance will be late, the helicopters will not be taking off, the launches between St. Mary's and the islands will not run. No matter how comfortable and civilised and prosperous life is on the islands, one has again that sense of the struggle, that realisation that the islands still are islands, that the sea around them is the enormous one of the Atlantic.

It will be clear then that in coming to the Isles of Scilly, you are coming, not to tropical gardens, not to South Sea islands in the wrong place, but to a granite appendix of Cornwall. There is not a dracœna around every turn in the lanes, or a prickly pear. You do not find yourself walking in an extended flower farm, among daffodils and mimosa and arum lilies. The climate is mild and warm. Strange plants can be grown, and are indeed grown, in the light sandy soil of the islands; but everything needs tending and protecting. A bulb field must be protected with hedges, must be placed, as far as possible, where the contours of the land give shelter and sunshine; and since such places are few, and the fields are small, and the islands add up into an extensive group, one quickly forgets the basic industry of the islanders, the articles on the bulb fields, and the photographs, and the newspaper stories.

Light is the energiser of the Isles of Scilly—a light sharper, clearer, giving more definition than the hazy light of the English mainland. Deprived of light by low clouds, the islands retreat into a dull bigness of sea; but when the clouds open and move away, when light surrounds and sharpens everything, gives colour to the sea, contrasts sea and land, what a medley it makes of detailed colour within a general subtlety of tones! In April, on a grey morning, even the vividness of gorse on an island half a mile away becomes scarcely a colour; and except for the autumn red of bracken, and the blues and greens of the water and its white splashes on the islets and isolated rocks, the dominant tones are quieter than the egg-yellow of gorse. The outcropping granite is not granite colour, grey or pink, but the pale grey, a greenish and a bluish grey in full light, of those lichens which grow around every boulder and fragment of stone. Lichens, grey lichens, grow among the herbage of the sandy flats and slopes. Lichens cover the gorse stems, the stems, as I have mentioned, of the wind-break shrubs, the trunks and branches of the few trees. The main greens of the island are greens mixed with grey, greens and grey mixed with pale browns. The sandhills are grey and blue with marram grass. The roads, unpaved except for the main roads of St. Mary's, are pale brown and grey.

These clarities of colour are speckled, permanently and according to the season, with all the illuminated detail—the occasional lights of orange lichen, the particular greens, from the sharp green of the fat leaves of mesembryanthemum crawling up rocks or sand dunes, to the darkish green of the leaves of daffodil and the rectangles of different darkness edging the fields.

Pittosporum hedges have different tones of olive, one dark, one silvery, an olive touched with blue, in contrast to the more ordinary greens, yellowish of the euonymus, dark of the veronicas, shiny of the escallonias. The pure specks of colour out of the watercolour box or the fabric pattern-book are scattered about everywhere—magenta against green of the mesembryanthemum flowers, blues of sea holly, blues of bugloss in the fields, the clear purple of vetch, the yellows of corn marigold, and of mullein, and of horned poppy on the sands. The white of the Mediterranean garlic (*Allium triquetrum*) on walls, hedges, banks, beside roads and paths, like a white bluebell, is succeeded by bluebells; and their blue is followed by the universality of cushions of sea pink, and the universality of foxgloves on the inhabited and the desert islands, the purple of heather, and mixed richness of the bracken. Areas of grassland are red with sorrel, a red matched by sheds roofed with pantiles, or with that galvanised iron burnt by the sea air. In the autumn, the grasslands and patches are spotted with toadstool whites and oranges and scarlets. In the autumn, too, one turns a corner to a patch of pink belladonna lilies alive under the sombreness of granite.

Since trees are so few, except for the pine plantations of St. Mary's and Tresco, the enormous light floods down on to all these colours, general and particular, in every hollow and upon every protuberance. The island surfaces away from the downs are uneven, so that colours are picked out with shadows; and the shadows have something of a Mediterranean sharpness. When the sun is down a bit, the green hedges of the bulb fields, or the granite walls are doubled with a black line. Each stone in the loose walls is edged with shadow in absolute clarity. Shadow defines the fleshy leaves and stems of the mesembryanthemum into a mottle of green and black.

All this is surrounded intricately with the altering blues of the sea—altering according to sky and tide and wind. Deep azure, silver azure, light blue-greens over sand, or deep azure turning to purple, from the underwater growth of weed around the rocks and islets. After the prevailing greens, or prevailing drabs of the mainland, the illuminated colours in a small area, or in a wide view from an island height, such as the Look Out on Tinkler's Hill, on St. Martin's, are a fantastic, luxurious refreshment for the eyes.

Wherever one may be on the islands, whatever island one may be on—since the islands float one after another beneath this great sky, and are not interrupted enormities of land—one stares into panoramas of sunset; sunsets of blinding yellow merging into green and blue, or sunsets immensely crimson. Moon rises are correspondingly rich. I recall coming from the Abbey at Tresco in September, on to a yellow full moon rising, a little squashed top and bottom, into a blue sky, out of a blue sea, divided from where I was standing by a deep sienna stretch of bracken. Though I have never seen it, I am told that after the sun has slipped below the sea, the phenomenon of the green ray often appears. And when the Northern Lights come, they are seen from the islands as from the best seats in the terrestrial theatre.

2
ISLAND HISTORY AND PREHISTORY

EVERY BOOK ABOUT SCILLY must take the archipelago island by island. But the separate islands need the preface of a more general picture of the group.

The islands and the rocks are fragments of a once continuous extent of granite eroded gradually into hill and hollow. Then in recent times the double effect of rising sea-level and a later tilting of the land mass lowered the Scillonian island, in the end by some thirty feet. The sea fretted in, and at last Scilly was divided into separate islands round a shallow lagoon. The sea worked along fissures in the granite running roughly west-north-west to east-south-east, as one can see from the Admiralty Chart. New and Old Grimsby Harbours and Crow Sound are aligned in this way. The islands themselves, Tresco, Tean, St. Martin's, Great Ganilly, Arthur, Annet, lie like narrow ridges more or less between these points of the compass. But as the land mass has sunk, so the Atlantic has created immense quantities of sand which make the bed of the lagoon, and heap up the dunes on the various islands, and prevent, I believe, some of the islands from being subdivided still further. Now and again (though geologists seem to have pushed this too far) the sand may have relinked, into one, islands which had already been divided.

If you take the two-inch map and colour it round the islands up to the five fathom line (depths between five fathoms and ten are not marked), you see how Scilly must have looked c. 2000 B.C., when first, so far as the evidence goes, it was certainly inhabited. The main group from St. Mary's in the south to Round Island in the north becomes one island. The sound would still separate St. Mary's from the combination of Agnes and the Gugh, and this united couple would still be divided—or almost divided—by Smith Sound from a larger Annet, running west to the Ranneys and south-west towards Melledgan. Most of the Western Rocks around Rosevear would unite into a fair sized island rather longer than Annet.

For all of this there is geological and archaeological evidence. Ancient walling runs under water, the sea covers prehistoric huts and burials, ferns suggesting "an old soil or land surface" have been found six feet down in digging a drain to reduce the pool on Agnes, and so on, in a complex of evidence (see Paul Ashbee's *Ancient Scilly*, 1974) which is being amassed and made to yield a not yet finalised picture. It is clear enough that four thousand years ago there would have been roughly double the existing land surface; which would have been capable of supporting a considerable population. The large number of megalithic graves and later barrows argue such a population, and speak of Scilly's position from the earliest days on the routes of trade and travel and migration between north-western continental Europe and Ireland, Wales and Scotland.

The final tilting of Scillonia did not come until late in the first centuries of our era. Romanised Britons in Scilly would have known more or less one principal island which still deserved a name in the singular. It remains usual to speak of "Scilly"; and perhaps by descent that "Scilly" is more than a convenient collective. "Siluram insulam" is how Scilly was mentioned by the Roman geographer Gaius Julius Solinus about 240 A.D. The monk and chronicler Sulpicius Severus about 400 A.D. wrote of "Sylinancim", again singular; and so it went on—"Sully", "Sullya" through the Middle Ages to our modern "Scilly" (in which the *y*, the Old Norse *ey*, "island", was added by the Vikings to the ancient and obscure main element).

Doubtful as many things continue to be about Scilly, archaeologists have now discerned rather more than an outline of its prehistory. A people who buried their dead in stone-walled, stone-roofed passage graves covered over with round stony barrows colonised Scilly not earlier than 1500 B.C. Belonging to the broad family of megalithic tombs, these graves are of a type now called 'chamber tombs', and their distribution makes it likely that the people who built them were seafarers from Finistère in Brittany. They have left a few chamber tombs in West Cornwall, scores in Scilly, and a few more on the coast near Waterford in the south-east of Eire. It is these megalithic people who were likely to have been the first inhabitants.

They used flint, which is abundant in Scilly, and bone for their harder implements, made pottery, thick and blackish and glittering with specks of mica, out of local clay, grew corn, and kept cattle and sheep; but also they ate great quantities of limpets, whose shells, which do not easily decay, make up most of the kitchen middens which they left in Scilly. The middens show, moreover, that they ate grey seal, wrasse and other fish, birds, and birds' eggs.

It would be wrong, no doubt, to imagine the Scilly they knew—or at least the large island they knew—as an unbroken area of low fertile soil out of which emerged the knobbly hills of granite. There must have been inlets of sea, and much of the central plain must have been marshy, looking like the flag-yellow marshes on St. Mary's between Hugh Town and Old Town and behind Porth Hellick. There would at least have been more abundant grazing for cattle—(ox bones of a very small breed, introduced no doubt after 1000 B.C., have been found in the middens)—and more abundant land for the small irregular plots of early agriculture, cultivated perhaps with the hoe and the digging stick. An iron descendant of the digging stick, similar to the Irish and Hebridean foot-plough, still survives in Scilly. Vegetation would not be dissimilar to the scrub on the desert islands such as Arthur or Northwethel, though oak trees, bent over with the wind, were probably abundant. (Oak tree roots have been dug up in the past, and charcoal from urns and middens and an Iron Age cist has been found to be of oak. Increasing exposure to salt winds as Scilly was divided, and the mediaeval introduction of rabbits, may have stopped the oaks from regenerating themselves.) The chamber tombs were small family tombs to begin with no doubt, in which the dead or their ashes were buried, and which could be opened and used again. As the centuries passed, the people of Scilly began to place their funeral urns in rectangular cists of granite slabs which were then closed, and sealed round with a barrow. But why has Scilly a surviving concentration of some fifty megalithic tombs against only two hundred for all of England and Wales? Hencken has suggested that Scilly had some especial sanctitude. Glyn Daniel thought of these builders of collective tombs as an isolated people who for centuries hardly changed the culture their Founding Fathers had brought with them to an uninhabited Scilly.

Later again—though the evidence is not conclusive—the "Scilly Culture", as it is now called, was modified still more by the arrival of those people who collected the burnt ashes of their dead into urns and buried them in the 'urnfields', usually without barrows, which can be traced back across Europe to the Danube. These urnfield people may or may not have been Celts, but from the Iron Age to the sixteenth century, it is safe to say that the islanders were predominantly Celtic, predominantly influenced in their ways and ideas from the Cornish mainland. The little cliff fort—the Giant's Castle—on St. Mary's is thought (*Antiquaries Journal*, Oct., 1941) to be a small version of the cliff-forts built by the Celtic Veneti in Finistère and the Morbihan—forts with multiple defences such as one finds also in Cornwall. Iron Age relics of the first century A.D. have occurred in Scilly (see the chapter on Tean), and to early Celtic speech may belong some of the island names which survived into the Middle Ages—Rentemen for the later Cornish Tresco, Bechiek or Brechiek for St. Martin's, Nurcho—though the identification is uncertain—for the Cornish Northwethel, Ennor for St. Mary's.

As Scilly, cleft gradually into its present items of land, goes forward into history, it becomes easier to chronicle the use of the islands from outside than the lives and character of the Scillonians. Roman remains consist of a few coins and an altar stone. In Celtic Christian times, in the sixth century, Welsh missionary saints who worked in Cornwall and Brittany founded small hermit-monasteries in the northern group of islands. Vikings made intermittent use of Scilly, leaving behind them a seafarers' place-name or two. King Athelstan took possession *c.* 937–939, no doubt for future security against the Dublin and Brittany Vikings. English hermits succeeded Celtic hermits, and under the crown, Scilly having become a royal property, their islands were controlled by the Benedictine monks of Tavistock Abbey, from the priory they built on Tresco. Throughout the Middle Ages and till the sixteenth century the thin record is mainly one of a few documents relating to the islands held by the monks, successors of the Celtic monks and hermits, a few grants of land in the secular islands to owners across the sea in England, a few ancient deeds as the tenements went from one owner to another, a few mentions of the castle on St. Mary's and of civil jurisdiction. Of the islanders themselves and daily life within the islands there is little enough trace. They were all of them, probably, inhabited—all of the major islands, except Annet and Arthur, and perhaps Great Ganilly. Life was insecure. The islands were ill-protected from the visiting ships of every nation, but rents and wreckage brought money to the landlords. They were cultivated, and the land, as it is now, was fertile. The many Cornish place-names suggest that islanders were mainly of Celtic or Cornish stock—a stock mixed no doubt by way of contact with shipping, contact with the Norsemen, and a closer connection with England ever since the tenth century. Yet the islands must have been Saxonised and Normanised to a degree, since the old Celtic dedications were supplanted and the memory of the Celtic saints decayed more thoroughly in the remote islands than in Cornwall itself.

It is from the time of the Tudors and the dissolution of the monasteries that the affairs of Scilly begin to abound in the state papers. Scilly became part of the Duchy of Cornwall. Wars and the expansion of trade began to give Scilly a new importance—an intermittent importance which has endured down to the second German war. Scilly had become, as indeed it remained for some time, a convenient haven for piracy, situated so plumply on the trade routes at the mouth of the English and Irish channels. The possession of Scilly by France or Spain became a •possibility against which precautions were needed. It was, wrote Sir Francis Godolphin to the Government, "the fairest inn in the direct way between Spain and Ireland". So after Henry VIII's war with France, Edward VI began the fortification of the islands; and Scilly remained fortified and garrisoned, in a desultory way, between wars, until the nineteenth century.

With Spain peering over the horizon, the work of Edward's reign was more energetically continued under Elizabeth. Tresco, guarding the northern entries into safe anchorages, and St. Mary's guarding the southern entries, were the two fortified islands, though there may have been minor breastworks of this time on the Gugh, and on Agnes at the southern entrance to Smith Sound. The fortification was pushed on by the Godolphin family from Cornwall. They became, and remained generation by generation, down to the eighteen-thirties, lessees of the islands under the Duchy of Cornwall, the lessee having the title of Lord Proprietor.

Since King Edward began his fort and blockhouses, much improvement had been made, tenements had been established and rough land had been enclosed, but in 1579 Francis Godolphin still found Scilly in a poor condition. The population had dwindled. Only the fortified islands of Tresco and St. Mary's were inhabited; besides women and children, there were only a hundred men, and there was no longer cultivated land enough to find bread for half of these few inhabitants. The Godolphins set about reforming these islands which they found "a bushment of briars and a refuge for pirates". Sir Francis Godolphin, according to the nice phrase in Carew's *Survey of Cornwall*, "by his Invention and Purse bettered his Plot and Allowance" in Scilly. He brought over new settlers from the mainland, and it was through him that Bryher and St. Martin's were repopulated. Judging from the place-names some of the new settlers were Cornish who still spoke Cornish. A few of the headlands have names beginning with the sixteenth-century Cornish *pedn-* for the older Cornish *pen-*. But many more of them were either not Cornish at all, or else Cornish who had given up their language. The older Cornish place-names are thickest on St. Mary's, which was never deserted, and on Agnes (which suggests that Agnes, despite Francis Godolphin's report of 1579, was not quite empty of the old island stock). On Bryher and St. Martin's, and a little less so on Tresco, the names are nearly all English, as though the old names had passed out of use and been forgotten.

The fortification of the islands under Sir Francis Godolphin (of which the chief remnants are Star Castle on St. Mary's and the Block House on Tresco) meant security at least for the islanders—a valuable security if one thinks of the

Flemish privateers and the North African rovers from Sallee, who preyed so fiercely upon English shipping in the seventeenth century. But it was too early to found a prosperous agriculture and solve the problems of wind protection in so exposed an archipelago. So the Scillonians were, and remained, for over two centuries, a community of men who lived as far as possible off their own land, who fished, earned money by skilful piloting in and out of the valuable havens of Scilly, and who added, later in the Godolphin dynasty, kelp-burning to their means of livelihood.

Scilly's connection with piracy must not be imagined in picturesque forms of pirate communities tucked away in the islands. Scilly was rather an occasional base, a haven for lurking just off the trade routes, where food and water could be taken on board, and where booty could be landed. One story of the seventeenth century piracy is told in full among Admiralty papers in the British Museum. It hints both at a common interest between Godolphin and his tenants and at some complicity in the trade among the Godolphins themeslves.

In 1603 a French merchant, Anthony Morier, came with a complaint to the Judge of the Admiralty Court in London. A year or so earlier he had loaded his ship the "Lewes Bonaventure," of a hundred tons burden, with almonds, nuts and other merchandise at Tarragona on the Mediterranean coast of Spain, and then left for Malaga in southern Spain. On the way the "Lewes Bonaventure" was boarded by an English captain and his company. After putting Morier and his crew ashore "in miserable estate" at Cap de Gata, they transhipped some of the cargo to their own vessel, and then took the "Lewes Bonaventure" across, conveniently to Barbary—Algeria, that is—and sold her with the rest of the cargo to their Moslem brothers in the trade. Then "the said pyrates" came with their almonds and nuts to Scilly "and there disposed unto Mr. Robert Penwarden the Lieutenant and divers other inhabitants there, the most parte of the foresaide Allmonds and nutts, wch being donne they disposed themselves ashore, somme in Cornwall and somme in Devon, and somme elsewhere." Morier asked for justice, after exhibiting proofs "of the spoyle aforesiad and of the cruell dealing" of the pirates towards him and his company; and then, armed with papers from London, began a disillusioning pilgrimage through the west. He was abused and disregarded at Plymouth by the Vice-Admiral of Devon, Sir Richard Hawkins, who released (the papers suggest bribery) some of the arrested pirates. Next he tried Sir Francis Godolphin himself at his house at Tavistock, and was sent over to Scilly to see Godolphin's son, the deputy governor. He arrived, and asked John Godolphin to arrest those islanders who had received the goods. "But the said Mr. Godolphin not only refused soe to doe but willed the complainant to departe giving him only a note of the names of somme few persons that had received (as they said) small quantities of his goods aforesaid and soe he departed." Back on the mainland he found one man he was after—the Scillonian Andrew Legg—brought him before Mr. Vivian, the Vice-Admiral of Cornwall, who sent the man on to Sir Francis Godolphin. Godolphin let Andrew Legg go, and accused Morier of "too much cruelty."

John Godolphin, it is true, had taken and signed some depositions about the almonds and hazel nuts (which had been brought into New Grimsby Harbour) from the islanders of St. Mary's, Tresco, Bryher and St. Martin's. Their statements were evasive and innocent; and were clearly accepted by John Godolphin, who, like everyone else, seems to have found the injured, persistent Frenchman a nuisance to be got rid of as quickly as possible, and with, at the same time, the least offence to London.

Under the Godolphins, and eventually under their descendants, the Dukes of Leeds, Scilly continued for more than two hundred years, until in 1834, a new lease and a new dynasty of Lords began with Augustus Smith. During the Commonwealth, when the islands, until Blake's reduction of them in 1651, were heavily garrisoned by Royalist troops and ships, Scilly had too many to feed, and suffered badly. St. Martin's was nearly depopulated once more, and Samson was deserted. Even the rabbit population was much reduced. For long after there was no one to interest himself in Scillonian welfare; and towards the end of the Godolphin dynasty, the Lord Proprietor's control had grown more and more distant, and his successive agents on St. Mary's had become more and more oppressive and independent. From as early as 1696, when a revenue station was established in the Scillies, the islanders had added smuggling to their livelihood—

smuggling from France and smuggling from ships (particularly West Indiamen) which increasingly used Scilly as a haven. Brandy was "sold so cheap" among the Scillonians, "that the poorest person can purchase it, to the injury of their health, the promotion of idleness, and the loss of the public revenue" (Troutbeck). By 1761, things were brisk enough for the customs controller to ask for arms for his men, and more than once there was bloodshed. The much sharper control, which was at last established between 1816 and 1819, contributed (with the salt tax, which made salt too dear for the salting in of winter fish) to the extreme impoverishment of the islanders, which reached its head in the famine on the "off islands" (the islands, that is, other than St. Mary's. The famine grew unnoticed under the noses of the Duke of Leed's representative and of the Lieutenant-Governor, who denied the existence of any distress, and was accused by the islanders' champion, the Rev. G. C. Smith, of being a drunken wretch who kept and debauched a Scillonian girl.

But it was in this distress that the later prosperity of the islands has been rooted, since it brought, from a mixture of romantic motives and Benthamite principles, the energetic, dictatorial Augustus Smith to Scilly; which he determined to reorganise and reform. And Augustus Smith and his successor carried with them into Scilly that "spirit of planting" which Borlase had found so miserably absent on his visit in 1752. Under Augustus Smith, a stern and single-minded bachelor, smuggling was stopped; the minute subdivision of holdings was done away with; surplus children were made to emigrate; roads, schools, quays, houses were built or rebuilt; new breeds of cattle and sheep were introduced, and farming improved. Emperor Smith had his way, little as the independent Scillonians like it, and little as their descendants like the memory of it today. Quoting from the "Song of Solomon," an old Scillonian once told Cecil Torr (who recorded it in his *Small Talk at Wreyland*) that Augustus "was terrible as an army with banners."

Augustus Smith had his private tastes and eccentricities—the botanical tastes which made him establish his garden of exotics on Tresco, the sporting tastes of the *grand seigneur* which made him introduce partridges, and turn Samson—from which he had sensibly removed the last few inhabitants—into a deer park (deer were also turned out on other islands), and the allied eccentricity of putting rabbits of different colours on the different uninhabited islands to mix with the grey population. He also bred ostriches, which stalked about on Tresco. There were limits rather to his omniscience than to his power. His farming does not seem to have been all that it might have been, and he can hardly have enjoyed reading an independent agricultural report in 1870 which ended by affirming that the ignorance of the farmers on many points of good systematic husbandry "might be remedied if the proprietor of the islands employed as his steward and as his bailiff, men well acquainted with the best methods of British farming."

Still, what was obvious and necessary he did, and he cast about for means to secure the livelihood of the islanders. Kelp-making had ceased early in his reign, though till the development of steamship-building and ship-owning grew profitably on St. Mary's. The export of potatoes was an old island trade, which Augustus Smith improved, making the islands concentrate on growing early potatoes, with a few other vegetable crops, chiefly asparagus. He changed farming into market-gardening. The flower trade began—just began—in his day, but rather by accident, than as the result of clear-cut intention. It began when Augustus Smith had a box of the various species of narcissus growing on the island sent up to Covent Garden. By the time he died in 1872, the industry was scarcely even an infant. It was under his successor, Thomas Algernon Dorrien-Smith, that it slowly extended and became the mainstay of the islanders, gradually ousting potatoes, and most of the remnants of the ancient farming of Scilly. It was under the second of the line of Smiths—"King Smith"—that the appearance of the islands began to change with the wind-break hedges of escallonia, euonymus, veronica, and pittosporum. Tamarisk, the other principal hedge plant, was of older growth in Scilly; but so late as 1870, the lower, less tender crops requiring no such careful protection, the field divisions were still granite, sometimes capped with sods, or planted on one side or both with furze.

Under Augustus Smith, the graph of island life mounted to viable poverty, and from poverty to prosperity. And it rose still more under his successors until the islanders desired control of their own affairs, and gained at last their own county

View of Higher Town, St. Martin's

council. The fourth of Augustus Smith's line is now lessee of Tresco alone among the inhabited islands. The lease of Tresco under the Duchy of Cornwall has ninety-nine years to run from 1929. Scilly was much indebted, no doubt, to the Benedictines of Tavistock in the early Middle Ages, much to Sir Francis Godolphin, but more (whether the Scillonians like admitting it or not) to Augustus Smith and his two successors who, were not merely Lords of Scilly, but Lords living in Scilly. Even Augustus might be surprised at the daily link to Cornwall by helicopter, and at the era of Aga cookers, flush lavatories, bathrooms, electric light plants, or wind generators, and smart motor-boats, in which the off-islanders live. There are obvious possibilities which may, in years ahead, reduce the prosperity of the Narcissus Age. But Scilly can never sink back to the old asperities of the Age of Limpets.

3

THE SCILLONIANS

CAN THERE BE any link between to-day's islanders and the Scillonians who built their megalithic chamber tombs, after colonising Scilly some four thousand years ago; or at least between modern Scilly and the Scilly of the Celtic settlers? Scilly has its own species of shrew, *Crocidura cassiteridum*, first described in 1924 from a specimen collected on the Gugh—belonging to a genus never found elsewhere, recent or fossil, in the British Isles (except in the Channel Islands, which nourish a different European species of *Crocidura*). Scilly has its own race of the Meadow Brown butterfly, but neither its indigenous plants nor its indigenous creatures are different otherwise from those on the mainland. And the flora of the uninhabited islands—except Tean and Samson—is much what it would have been primævally —it is a flora "almost certainly the least contaminated by human hands of any to be found in the South of England" (J. E. Lousley in *The Journal of Botany*, July, 1939).

But new people, new plants, new insects, have entered Scilly. The Scillonians are certainly a diverse mixture—as mixed, if one could divide out all the constituents of their make-up, as all the assembly of garden plants and of immigrant weeds that flourish in the bulb fallows. Their more recent ancestors have included garrison soldiers, Royalists who clung to Scilly until 1651, settlers from the mainland at various dates (in and after the Second World War several marriages took place between islanders and land-girls who had volunteered for work in Scilly), chance comers from shipping and probably from wrecks. In 1709, there was a proposal to find homes in Scilly for four hundred and fifty of the German protestant refugees from the Palatinate, but if any came, and I have found no record of it, they were certainly not the full four hundred and fifty, who would have preserved their *Deutschtum* as the Palatine refugees preserved it for long among the Irish. Still, the islanders are a mishmash by descent. There are families, especially in St. Mary's, who claim to be descended from the sixteenth century Godolphins. One St. Martin's man believes that his ancestor was an outward bound emigrant, so seasick that he begged to be put ashore on the first land the ship came to. The ship took shelter off St. Martin's, and there he was landed with his trunk. Other Scillonians are the children and grandchildren and great-grandchildren of employees brought over by Augustus Smith and Thomas Algernon Dorrien-Smith to the Home Farm on Tresco.

Yet since the islands, so far as one knows, were never wholly depopulated, there may be some frail vein of consanguinity running back from the present able, healthy, quickwitted stock to the inhabitants of prehistory. Certainly that stock is now becoming ill adapted, or less adapted in the old ways, to the stringencies and peculiarities of island life, as those stringencies in some degree diminish. One Scillonian, talking about his smuggling ancestors, remarked that the islanders once thought nothing of taking a six-oared gig across to the French coast, but now they wanted an outboard motor for going from St. Mary's to Tresco, and diesel engines for a trip to Penzance. The man who fishes for a living is not extinct, but for each score of men who knew, sixty years ago, every ledge around Scilly there are now perhaps two. But then the islanders do not live so much off, or out of, the sea as they were compelled to a hundred years ago. Earlier visitors have remarked how much the Scillonians seemed without traditions and folklore which were rooted in the islands themselves—not so surprising seeing how the stock was added to continually. Yet the observations were exaggerated. They had, and still have perhaps, their fag-ends of superstition; but so have we on the mainland, and in more abundance.

Small black cattle, often mentioned by the early writers, survived until Augustus Smith introduced the present cross-breds. Sheep, "an interesting and picturesque, but far from useful breed" with "white heads, straight thin noses, short ears, and small bright eyes," with crooked backs, and ragged tails and loose shining wool, led a "goat-like existence among their native rocks"— including the rocks of the desert islands. It is engaging to think that in these black cattle and sheep, both inured to the eating of seaweed, there may have been a strain of the ancient small oxen and the sheep whose bones have been found in the kitchen middens. The black cattle must have resembled the little black Kerries of Ireland, survivors of the Celtic ox. The sheep were obviously akin to the Soay sheep of Harris and the Faroes and elsewhere, descendants of the turbary sheep of Neolithic Britain. But such sheep and cattle could well have been brought over under Francis Godolphin in the sixteenth century; and the island sheep, from which the Scillonians spun their yarn and wove their cloth, sound much like the old unimproved Cornish breed. A continuity has been remarked, though one would hesitate to be too sure about it, between the methods of prehistoric walling on the islands and the modern methods of building a wall of granite. But the Scillonians' dependance upon the natural products of Scilly has immensely lessened within the last half-century. Vernacular building in granite has gone, thatch has nearly gone. Sheep vanished a year or two before 1939. One can even eat fish brought over on the steamer from Penzance. Pillas, the rye-like cereal grown also in Cornwall and no doubt brought over from Cornwall, went long ago out of cultivation, although curiously a little rye is still grown on St. Martin's, and still threshed by beating the sheaves over the edge of a barrel. Rye, moreover, is held to have been scarce in Britain until Anglo-Saxon times.

Perhaps one could fairly sum the Scillonians up by saying that they are a people without a history, living on islands whose history was made from the outside. Even the English they speak lacks a marked peculiarity—another of the facts noted from the eighteenth century. Yet one can trace in it, not unnaturally, a tinge of Cornish dialect and dialectical usage; and a collection of island words—never yet made so far as I know, though there are several still in use—might reveal the islanders' linguistic kinship with Cornwall. What the islanders have perforce is an island constitution of mind, a leisureliness and an indifference to the urgencies of mainland life, which a visitor, desperately trying to get to his lodging on one of the off-islands at the wrong time, may find a bit irksome. And some of the inescapable restrictions of island life, particularly on Bryher, Anges, and St. Martin's, mean that the small populations of those islands must continue to live less individually and privately, and more as a community, than we have come to live in mainland villages.

The Scillonians as a group are more homogeneous than they were. They intermarry more between islands, mix together more in amusements; but still it would not be true to say that the last peculiarities which distinguish a Bryher man from an Agnes man, and both from the native of St. Martin's, or the native of the privately-managed Tresco or the cosmopolitan St. Mary's, have altogether been smoothed away. Bryher still has its large clan of Jenkinses, St. Martin's its clan of Bonds, Agnes its clan of Hickses (twelve out of an electoral roll of forty-three). In 1651 Hicks was already the chief name on Agnes, Jenkinses lived on Tresco and St. Martin's, though not on Bryher. Bonds introduced themselves later. Watts, Legg and Christopher are other names found now and three hundred years ago. Each group is faithful to its own island, and Bryher, St. Martin's and Agnes have a conservatism which is still discernible.

Yet so far as they possess it in common, the

Scillonians have, and cannot escape their own insular character, in its virtues and its demerits. The character modifies and alters in some points. But it cannot, so long as the basic ownership of Scilly remains, be swamped into uniformity with England. Most of the land is still held from the Duchy, which is jealous—and properly jealous—of letting in too many mainlanders, except on holiday.

4

TRESCO AND NORTHWETHEL

TRESCO AND ST. MARY'S, in the record of Scillonian affairs, have divided between them as much celebrity as the islands, one by one, have ever possessed. As I have pointed out, they may be the only islands in the group which have never been depopulated and empty since Scilly was divided into pieces.

Yet when Augustus Smith came to Tresco and started to build his mansion at that point from which nearly the whole archipelago can be surveyed, Tresco had not profited much from its centuries of continuous settlement. There was a church, there were houses, there were fortifications, there were the few ruins of the priory where the Tresco people still buried their dead; but there was more possibility than achievement. Nothing, Augustus Smith recorded, nothing grew in Tresco above the height of a gorse bush, except in the garden of the small parsonage which the S.P.C.K. had built for its island missionary. So the appearance of the island, even more than the appearance of its neighbours, comes from the alterations made by Augustus Smith, and the two succeeding members of his line. Augustus Smith made the first plantations, the roads, the quays (Tresco has no less than three, one on each side of the island, and one for low tide approach at Carn Near). He and his successors built the newer cottages, and the school, and rebuilt the church, as they built so much on the rest of the islands when they still held an undiminished lease. They discovered, bit by bit, by experiment, failures, successes, accident, how to utilise the mild temperature of Scilly, and how to turn its poverty into comfort.

Augustus Smith planted trees first of all—however unusual a specimen of the kind, he was a country gentleman from the mainland—to form a cover for game behind the ruins of the priory. He started with elm, sycamore, oak, and poplar. He planted shelter belts of ilex, cypress, and the Monterey Pine from California; and behind them he began the celebrated gardens. It was his nephew, Thomas Algernon Dorrien-Smith, who solved the wind-break problem, and hit upon the importance of the Monterey Pine above other trees. Coming up channel after a severe storm he noticed a tree standing among many which had blown down "He took a bearing on it and found it to be *Pinus radiata* (*insignis*)"—so realising its peculiar value in rooting itself into the shallow Scillonian soil. (The story is told by Bishop Hunkin, in "Tresco Under Three Reigns," Part I, *Journal of the Royal Horticultural Society*, May, 1947). This is the tree which muffles so much of Tresco in low dark green, and which has been planted here and there (but sparsely, as if the islanders were indifferent to improvement beyond a certain point) on the other islands. It resists salt, and stands up, as well as anything can do so, to the incessant winds by which the Scillies can be harassed. Luckily, it does not get frost, though its dark needles were sorely touched in 1947 and 1962–1963.

The pines, the gardens, the Abbey, and some of the modern building (which has not always been a shapely change from the vernacular of the Scillies) make Tresco peculiar among its fellows. Not everyone likes the peculiarity, or puts Tresco high in his scale of the Isles of Scilly. Yet even if one's eyes persist in being true to what they receive and prefer—for example, the gorse and heather and hilliness and granite hardness of Bryher—one should still be grateful for the boldly romantic endeavour which has created the modern Tresco.

It has been the personal side, as I have mentioned earlier, of a deliberate and remarkable and adventurous social experiment; and if Augustus Smith made the gardens for himself, he and his successors have always allowed the world to enter them. Moreover, out of the gardens, out of the ceaseless, enthusiastic cultivation of new plants from the southern hemisphere, many of the things have spread around which please one's eye in Scilly, and have been of admirable service to the islanders. To name only four plants, the mesambryanthemums, the *Pittosporum crassifolium*, exquisite in its growth and foliage as well as the quickest growing of wind-breaks, the tall blue *Echium*, and the Belladonna lilies, which glow so unexpectedly in granite-guarded corners in the autumn—all of these have had their first home around the Abbey (though certainly, one exotic, the American Aloe, grew in the garrison on St. Mary's before Augustus Smith's invasion).

How much one can appreciate the gardens themselves depends upon one's degree of curiosity and love of plants. Myself, I find the soft floor of the pine woods, the noise of the pines in the wind, the criss-crossing angles of their trunks, the emergence from their atmosphere on to distances of sand and sea, not among the least delights of the islands. And there is one place under the pines which is lit in the autumn by a soft red wattle, as well as by the yellow wattle—the "mimosa"—of London shops.

Still, pines, gardens, Abbey and all, Tresco remains Tresco—remains an island native to its group. Tresco cultivated is best seen in low, clear sunlight from a boat somewhere around Menavaur, in the Atlantic. It is the tender view of Tresco—the gentle green folds and slopes rising like a park, with the Block House fort behind them; and, running along the sky, edging the illuminated green, the low darkness of the pines.

Tresco's natural distinction among the other islands is to have the longest tranquillities of sand. The other big islands have their coves and curves of sand, but nothing stretching so far as the eastward beaches of Tresco from Block House, around little headlands to Lizard Point, from Lizard Point to Skirt Island—lonelinesses of sand, sloping up into sandhills bound by blue marram-grass. The distance from Block House to Skirt Island is only a mile and a bit over; but in Scilly one's scales of bigness and littleness are altered; and a mile of sand is like five miles along the southern coasts of Wales, or around the Gower peninsular.

Figure Heads, Tresco

I would as soon bathe, and laze, and sleep and watch the shrill oyster-catchers in their black, white and scarlet, and hunt for pink cowries along this white mile as along any beach I know. And as the tide creeps up, one's being can extend smoothly across the inland sea, over St. Martin's Flats, to the long, sun-intercepting ridge of St. Martin's. George Woodley (who wrote, after all, the Scillonian book which most combines intelligence, observation and long acquaintanceship with the islands) also wrote peoms, and found an authentic phrase or two now and then in verse as in prose. Worse has been written than his 'Sunset at Scilly':

. . . The west-wind rippled the dilating surge,—
   (A shivered mirror) and disturbed the glare
That, when no gales old Ocean's bosom urge,
   Settles in vast and dazzling richness there.

Before me smiled the wide-expanded main,—
   Concealing snares and death!—like worldly
      smiles!
And,—dotting thick the azure-tinted plain,—
   On either side, brown rocks and swelling
      Isles . . .

Woodley was looking the other way, it is true, looking west towards the sun; but it is an azure plain—an azure plain broken and given perspective by rocks—that one wanders across by eye from the Tresco beaches.

In prehistoric remains Tresco is barest of all the big islands. Hencken mentions only one chamber tomb, at the far north of the island, where, on

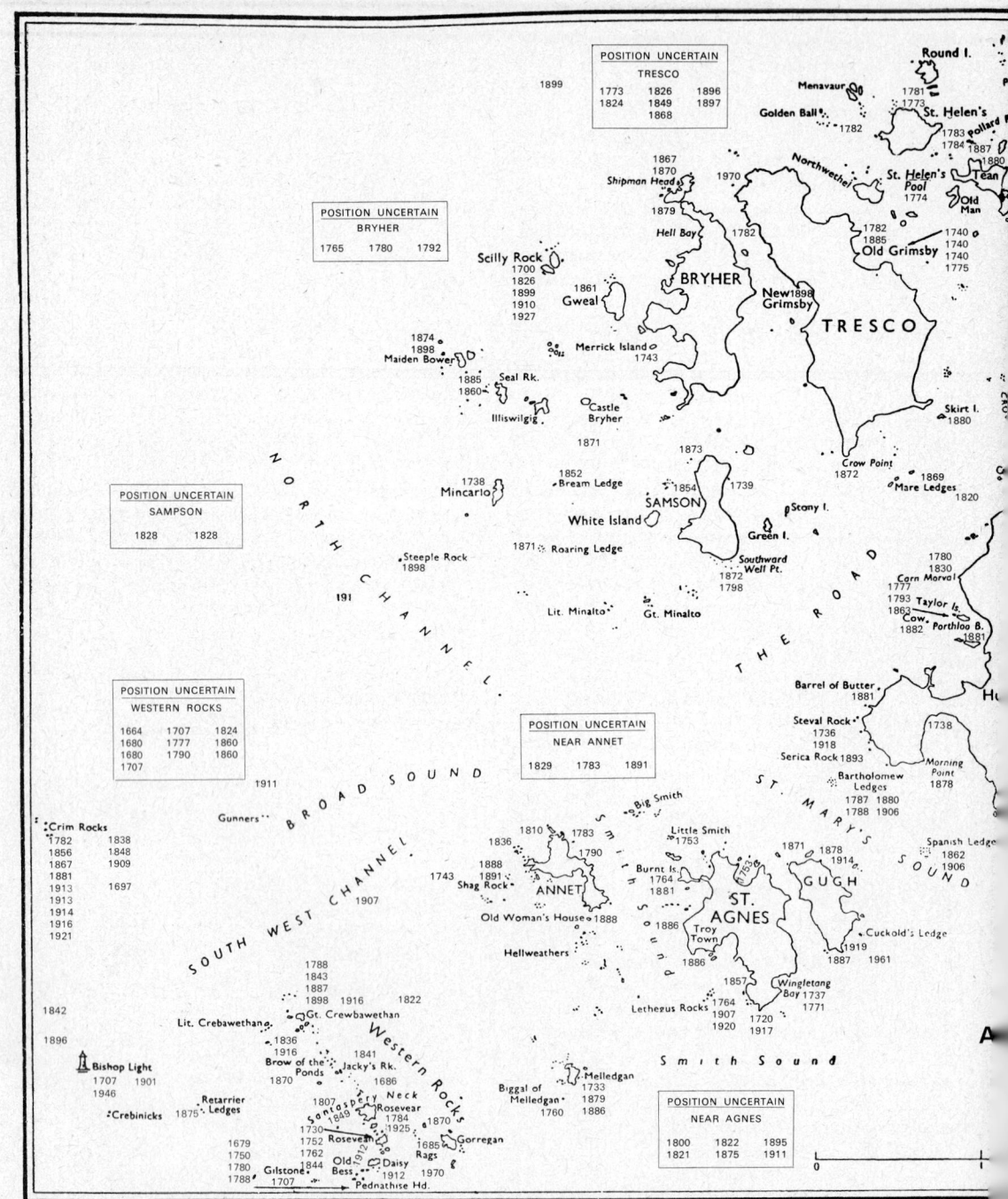

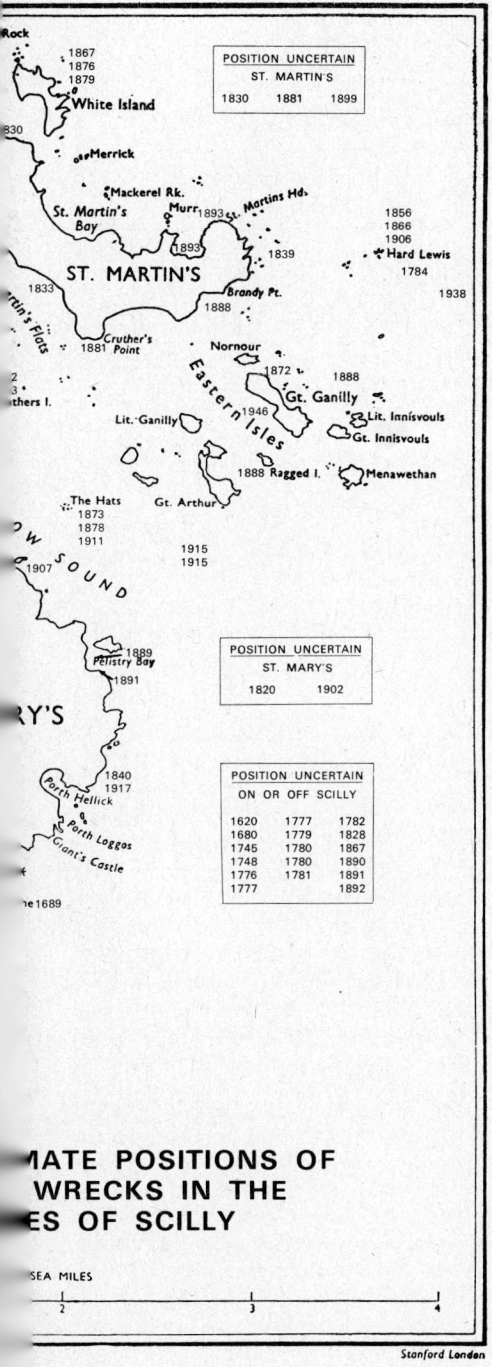

Castle Down, as on Shipman Head Down, barrows are plentiful, unopened and not worn down to any passage or cist they may contain. Woodley believed that he saw a large stone circle on the hill north of the Abbey Pond. The circle had a diameter of 160 yards. In the centre "is a group of romantic rocks, and a person standing on one of these must be visible to nearly the whole island." But—"the circle has lately been broken in upon, and several of the stones have been removed, to form some enclosures on the hill." Cists have certainly been found, and I have heard of limpet middens. Still, this archæological barrenness is not surprising. Next to St. Mary's, Tresco has had for a very long time the largest population; in Woodley's day nearly five hundred people lived there. The mediæval priory, and whatever church or oratory preceded the building which still remains in two arches and a few stones, the sixteenth- and seventeenth-century fortifications, three quays, the modern Abbey—add the builders of them all to the generations who have farmed on Tresco, and then ask where the megaliths have gone. Round about 1870 the downs on Tresco were being "rapidly improved—the surface rocks removed by blasting, the furze uprooted, and grass seeds sown."

Tresco's datable record, then, in the hewn solidity of stone begins with the priory—which has been inaccurately known for at least some three hundred years as "The Abbey." Yet it begins, not with the priory ruins, which are thirteenth-century work (and so not as old as the Romanesque arch in the Old Church on St. Mary's), but with a stone in the priory ruins, inscribed—(no more is legible under the masonry of the doorway arch)—

THI FILI
COG

in Roman capitals. The time it belongs to is the fifth or sixth century, and by analogy it is likely to be a Christian tombstone—dating, in fact, from the missionary age of the Welsh saints. I shall deal a bit more with the saints connected with Scilly—Samson, Ilid, Maudetus, Theona—in the chapter on St. Helen's, but everything suggests it was Tresco and not St. Helen's which was the chief centre of the Celtic, as later of the Roman Church, in the islands. Tresco parish is still held to include Northwethel, St. Helen's, Tean, Round Island and

Map by Captain Greenville Collins 1693 loaned by P. J. Radford, Fareham

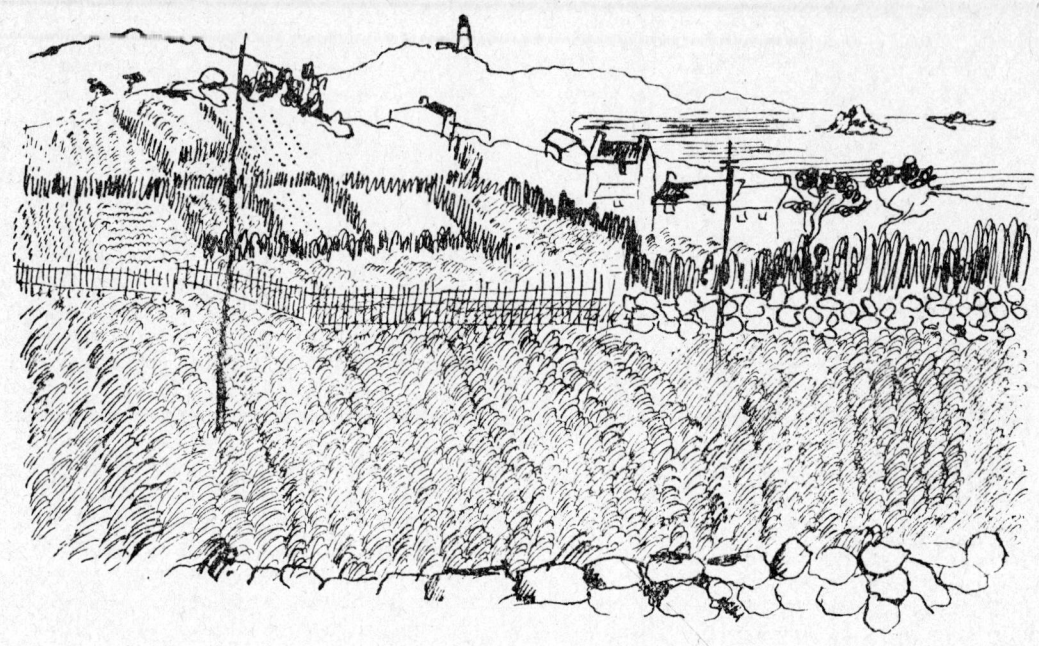

Tresco, overlooking Old Grimsby

Samson; and it must be these islands which formed what the Cornish antiquary Charles Henderson presumed to be the "religious group" possessed by "a confederacy of hermits" (*Cornish Church Guide,* p. 194). Henry I granted to Tavistock Abbey the churches in Scilly, with their possessions and land "as the monks or better hermits held it in the time of Edward the Confessor and Burgold Bishop of Cornwall." Reginald, Earl of Cornwall, confirmed the right of wreckage to the monks of Scilly in Rentemen, Nurcho, and the isles of St. Elidius, St. Samson, and St. Theona. A papal bull in 1193 confirmed Tavistock Abbey in their possessions, naming the islands as St. Nicholas, St. Samson, St. Elidius, St. Theona, and Nutho. Rentemen—the name never occurs again—must be Tresco, later called St. Nicholas, after the patron saint of the priory which the Benedictines of Tavistock established. And it is fair to look for Nutho or Nurcho among the other islands in Tresco parish (the linking of Tresco and Bryher as a Conventional District, Bryher being served by the Priest in Charge of Tresco, is a modern arrangement). Tean, Samson, and St. Helen's being ruled out, one is left with Round Island and Northwethel; and as monks, or human beings, in the absence of lighthouse buildings, can hardly have lived on Round Island, the probable possibility is that Nutho or Nurcho and Northwethel are one.

Besides Samson, Ilid, and Theona, no other island in Scilly bore the name of a Celtic saint except the "St. Maudut" of a document of 1336 (G. H. Doble: *St. Mawes*, 1938). St. Maudut, as a saint, is identified with St. Mawes of the mainland, St. Modez, or St. Maudetus, of Brittany, where his foundations were within St. Samson's bishopric. Doble thought "St. Maudut" was the island of St. Martin's. But it may have been Northwethel, its saintly against its secular name. Or it may even have been Tresco, since Tresco is likely to have had the *llan* or monastic cell of a Celtic saint, before the Anglo-Saxon hermits took possession and before Tavistock set up the priory of St. Nicholas.

There is a limit to speculation, and I have not been able to trace the document Canon Doble referred to. But at least it is not speculative that early and mediæval Christianity on the islands centred mainly on Tresco.

Names of more than one of the northern islands in Scilly have chopped and changed. St. Elidius's Island, *insula Sancti Elidii* in 1193, kept its name with slight variation, at least to the sixteenth century. By 1650 it had become St. Helen's. St. Martin's is a name unrecorded before Leland round about 1540. Surmise amounting to certainty makes it the Bechiek or Brechiek of fourteenth-century documents. Tresco, the earlier "Rentemen," was St. Nicolas in 1193, and Trescau by 1305 (*tre* "homestead" plus *scaw* "elder"—"elder tree homestead"). It may also preserve its Norse name in New and Old Grimsby ("Grymsey" in 1570—"probably Old Norse *Grims ey*—'Grim's Island,' the later form due to association with Grimsby (Lincs). Less likely, Old Norse *Grims by* —'Grim's town.' Almost certainly Scandinavian and probably the O.N. name for Tresco").

The earlier books have little of great moment to record of Tresco. Woodley thought that the "forest of Guffaer," within which the Scillonian monks were confirmed by King John in the tithe of three cleared acres, was the area known in his day (and still so called, and now planted with trees once more) as "The Abbey Wood." Possibly—though it is curious that the monks should need confirmation of tithes in a part of their own island. Admiral Blake's troops fought their path across Tresco in the April of 1651, coming in from Tean and Northwethel, storming, it appears, and burning what was left of the priory church.

Other things to note on Tresco are, that "Cromwell's Castle" is not incorrectly named: it was built immediately after the surrender of the islands in 1651; that Piper's Hole is anything but a dull sea-cavern; that the great troughed oval of granite was part of a horse-driven corn-mill, and not, as guide books say, a cider-mill.

The twelve unfriendly acres of Northwethel are easily enough visited from Old Grimsby on Tresco. Rough, rocky, matted with a deep pile of grass and brambles, the island has sharp and awkward shores, though a curved beach below the flat portion of the island opens on to St. Helen's Pool. I have already hazarded that Northwethel was the early Nutho or Nurcho, and was one of the confederacy of hermit islands, small and barren as it is. Yet the island flat could have been cultivated; and the character of the island would seem different if the flat were covered with smooth turf, instead of a deep tangle which swallows and tears at one's legs. In the sixteenth century, and later, one finds Northwethel called "Arworthel" or "Arworthill." It may be a corruption of a name containing the Cornish *ar,* 'on,' 'upon' plus the diminutive of *goerth* or *gwith*, a 'vein' or 'channel.' The island, in fact, bounds the four to five fathom channel, by which ships came in from the north-west to the anchorage of Old Grimsby. It lies so close to Tresco that provisioning a Northwethel hermit would not have been very difficult, except during a north-westerly gale.

The 25-inch map marks no less than ten barrows on Northwethel, nine of them at the south-eastern end, where one looks across the water to the ruined blockhouse on Tresco and to Tresco's eastern shores. In one of the barrows is a chamber tomb crossed by two capstones. One can trace a little ridge wall between the chamber tomb and the natural granite behind, on the next high point.

But there is at least one other piece of human handiwork on Northwethel which needs some examining and explaining. Not far from the entrance grave a wall runs out to a piled headland of granite. Naturally walled by this granite on two sides, and artificially walled on the other two sides, a little, roughly rectangular enclosure is tucked away into shelter. Temptingly one thinks of a Celtic monk or Saxon hermit. Then again, of a small sheep pen, since sheep were certainly pastured on Northwethel, then of the Parliamentarian attack upon Tresco. On the April day when the attack opened, three companies of men were left on Northwethel "to keep the Enemy busie," while the rest, after the failure of this first assault, were anxiously disembarked upon Tean. The little enclosure could easily have been roofed over and the two artificial walls quickly thrown up. It would have protected its occupants from stray shots across the water fired by the Royalists from Tresco.

When the first attack was delivered, with Admiral Blake's ships lying off-at-sea, the soldiers had been thwarted by ignorance and tide—ignorance especially of a Cornish pilot. "Accounted the most knowing Pilot for the place," he misdirected the commanders on to Northwethel. He had assured them that Northwethel, as it can indeed appear to be from a boat, was part of Tresco. The three companies who were not withdrawn can hardly have enjoyed more comfort on Northwethel than their companions did, nearly waterless and without provisions, across the Pool on the rather larger and kinder island of Tean.

5

ST. HELEN'S

OF THE REAL ISLANDS, distinct from rocks, the three most northerly are White Island, Round Island (which is a rock with a flat top) and St. Helen's; and St. Helen's a high lump of 144 feet, sloping up quickly from St. Helen's Pool opposite Tean, Old Man and Northwethel, is an island to be visited archaeologically, rather than scenically; though the summit (where there seem to be remains of an unrecorded chamber tomb) gives a wide survey of the islands. St. Helen's has a small rock-walled sandy harbour, cleared and roughly quayed below the granite and red brick pest-house.

By an Act of Parliament in 1756, ships north of Cape Finistère, with the plague or similar infection on board, had to proceed to St. Helen's Pool for quarantine. Two years before, an Act had established the quarantine station in New Grimsby Harbour, between the inhabited islands of Tresco and Bryher. Against this the islanders naturally protested to Lord Godolpin, arguing the superiority and greater safety of St. Helen's Pool, surrounded by islands which were not inhabited. The change was made, and ships not infrequently came in for quarantine—to the annoyance, no doubt, of all the other ships, particularly those engaged on the Chester and the Irish trade, which turned the now lonely St. Helen's Pool into a frequented anchorage. It was also the anchorage of a sloop stationed in Scilly during the Napoleonic Wars—presumably the sloop *Hornet*, whose commander lies buried under the floor of the Old Church on St. Mary's:

> Underneath
> Are deposited the remains of
> LIEUT. CHARLES WILLIAMS
> who was commander of
> H.M. SLOOP THE HORNET
> Guard ship at St. Helen's Pool
> He departed this life
> On the 8th day of August
> 1810
> Aged 37 years.

The Pest House itself is a plain, sturdy ruin, a human annotation to the island, which gives a welcome as one disembarks. But the Pest House (its chief use has been to provide the ordnance surveyors with something obvious and durable for a bench mark), and its well, and its quay, are nothing to the perhaps invisible group of buildings and walls some two hundred yards eastward along the flat above the Pool; which brings one back to the sanctitude of the northern islands.

I say invisible, because unless one is lucky, and the island has recently been burnt off, these buildings, or foundations of buildings, will be concealed under a tough, sharp, spongy mixture of thorns and grass. After a German raider had lit up St. Helen's with incendiaries during the war, the foundations were mapped, and the map and the findings—surface findings—published in the *Antiquaries' Journal* (October, 1941).

What the plan indicated was a small monastery of the Celtic Church—within its rough temenos walls, monks' cells, an oratory and a hermit's cell. The plan was compared with that of the Celtic monastery on Ynys Seiriol, off the coast of Anglesea. The typical enclosing wall served, at least symbolically, to shut out the sight of the world and so direct the vision and the mind of the monks upward, to higher things.

The monastery was no doubt one of several on the islands around Tresco. Here, in the foundation of St. Ilid, or Elidius, the saint himself might have joined the monks in occasional retreat. Here in Anglo-Saxon times lived, no doubt, one of the hermits mentioned in Henry I's grant to the Abbey of Tavistock. The other monks, and the hermits after them, would have lived on Tresco, on Tean, on Northwethel, and upon Samson, where the ruins of St. Samson's oratory were still plain in the last century. Everything points to an island group of Celtic foundations in the sixth century, similar to the group on the islands off the Bay of Saint-Brieuc, on the west of Brittany, where St. Maudetus had a foundation on Ile Modez and St. Samson on Ile de Brehat. Whatever saint it first belonged to, the foundation on Tresco, succeeded by the little priory of St. Nicholas, may have been the most important, although St. Samson and St. Maudetus were saints eminent above most. But it was St. Ilid whose island monastery was succeeded by a little mediaeval chapel, whose sanctity seems to have been most durable in the islands, remembered in 1448, when William of Worcester was on his travels, and in Henry VIII's time nearly a century later, when Leland, mistaking St. Ilid's sex, made his note of "Sanct Lides isle wher yn tymes past at her sepulchre" (as if the saint was buried here) "was gret superstitution."

St. Ilid is not so faint a figure as St. Theona, of Tean. He had foundations in Wales, and possibly in Brittany, and two mediaeval chapels in Cornwall bore his name, one in the extreme east, in St. Mellion parish, one towards Scilly in the extreme west, at Cape Cornwall. Besides St. Ilid, St. Samson, St. Maudetus and St. Theona, one may add to the tradition of the Celtic sanctitude of the islands that Nicholas Roscarrock, the Elizabethan poet, Catholic, and reverencer of the Cornish saints, had seen St. Mawgan mentioned as "Bishop of the Iles of Scilly."

What had shown on the surface at St. Helen's in 1941, or in 1947 when the island was burnt off a second time, couldn't be accurately interpreted. Then in the nineteen-fifties the little monastery complex within its wall was cleared and excavated (*Archaeological Journal, CXXI*, 1964), revealing an oratory and round hut, three more or less square huts, chapel, and a number of graves near the chapel doorway. The round hut and the little oratory were the two earliest buildings.

When Borlase came to the islands in 1752, and when John Troutbeck, Chaplain of the Islands, partly lifting the words of Borlase's description, wrote of it in his *Survey* in 1796, the mediaeval chapel, at least, was not ill preserved. The walls and the windows were standing, and the two internal arches, which Borlase called "of uncouth style." This, in his mid-eighteenth century idiom, needs to be interpreted as Romanesque. Borlase drew the arches, and the drawing in his manuscript (which he did not include among the engravings in his book) shows them to have been well shaped and neat. There were still abundant ruins at the time of the Napoleonic Wars, when, says Woodley, the commander of one of His Majesty's sloops (perhaps he was the Lieutenant Williams I have mentioned) "caused a great many of the stones to be taken away to make a *hedge* for his garden on an adjoining spot! Thus the desecration of the temples is not alone to be attributed to Vandals, Goths and Huns!"

The position had been a pleasant one for meditating hermits or monks—in good weather—, sheltered, sunny, intimately tucked between the high ground, most of it on a gentle slope, and St. Helen's Pool. It seems both lonely and friendly, like the spot where the oratory or chapel once stood on Samson. In his *Celtic Miscellany* Kenneth Jackson translates a wonderful Irish hermit poem of the twelfth century, in which St. Columba is supposed to be speaking about his island hermitage—in terms which would do exactly for St. Ilid here in Scilly:

Delightful I think it to be in the bosom of an isle . . . that I might often see there the calm of the sea.

That I might see its heavy waves over the glittering ocean, as they chant a melody to their Father of their eternal course . . .

That I might hear the sound of the shallow waves against the rocks; that I might hear the cry by the graveyard, the noise of the sea.

That I might see its splendid flocks of birds over the full-watered ocean; that I might see its mighty whales, greatest of wonders . . .

It is tempting, as one surveys the site from among the foxgloves and mesembryanthemum on the higher slope of St. Helen's, to assume that the events recorded in the 'Heimskringla' took place within this sanctified enclosure, though it might as well have been on Tresco or Samson or on Tean. Olaf Tryggvason, here in Scilly, towards the end of the tenth century, visited a Christian hermit and soothsayer, who foretold both the glories of his reign and—again rightly—the events of the next few hours. He learnt Christianity of the hermit and was baptised before he left the islands.

There is little else to record of St. Helen's and its forty-nine rough acres, beyond the black rabbits and the field enclosures near the Pest House. These may be the remains of seventeenth-century cultivation, for there is at least one statement—the statement of an accurate observer—suggesting that St. Helen's was occupied for a time, at least, after the neglect and ruination of the church. In 1669 Count Lorenzo Magalotti came to the Scillies with his master, Cosmo III, Grand Duke of Tuscany, whose ship took shelter in St. Mary's Road on his journey from Ireland to Plymouth. In Magalotti's *Travels of Cosmo III,* of which the English portion was translated and published in 1821, he says that St. Mary's, St. Martin's, Tresco, St. Agnes, Samson and "St. Hellena" were inhabited: "On each of the last two there is only a single family which, beside an adequate number of cattle, cultivate as much land as is capable of affording them an abundant sustenance." But no one lived on St. Helen's when Scilly was surveyed for the Parliament in or after 1651.

6

TEAN

TEAN (you pronounce it Teän) comes next among the sanctified islands; and if you look down at Tean from the high ground of Tinkler's Hill on St. Martin's, you see a flattish island roughly crescent-shaped, the two horns pointing southward into the lagoon. Between the two horns are two curved beaches, backed by sandy stretches of grass, which are free of bracken and brambles, since Tean—the last link with its human occupation—has always been grazed, and is still grazed, by cattle. Midway in the crescent and lying back from the grass flats is the Great Hill of Tean, a slope of gorse ending in granite, a hundred feet high. On either side of it are smaller hills.

The desert islands have each a pronounced character—friendly and unfriendly. Tean's character is an open and friendly one. It was an island likely to attract inhabitants; and certainly it was inhabited for a very long time, from a very early period. There are burial mounds on Great Hill, there is a chamber tomb on Old Man, one of the horns of the crescent, and a separate island at the highest tides. There is a well in the waist of the island under Great Hill, fitted now with a pump for the cattle. The water has a murky taste, and needs to be boiled. On the seaward side of this well, which was there three centuries ago, on a point of land between the two beaches of East Porth and West Porth, stands a thatched granite cottage, used as a cattle shed. Heavy granite walls at right angles protect it from the sea.

It was this cottage which housed the Mr. Nance who introduced kelp-burning to Scilly in 1684 and settled on Tean, which he leased, and which his descendants long continued to lease, jealously, from the Lord Proprietor. He was a Cornishman from Falmouth, and came over to Scilly to establish an independent business, having already relations with the manufacturers at Gloucester, to which, with Bristol, most of the Scillonian kelp was exported. If one scratches about on the foreshore, to the right of the doorway, one finds where the women of the house, with a fling of the right hand, threw their rubbish. I have unearthed fragments of cups, plates, earthenware bowls, glass, coal ashes, bones, and a broken spindle whorl of red and black pottery. Most of the bits belong to the seventeenth century, some of them, coloured scraps of industrial pottery from Staffordshire, show that the cottage was inhabited on and off at least a hundred years later, and for a good many generations after the death of the original Nance from the mainland—inhabited no doubt at the kelp-making season. Ten people, two "able to carry arms," comprising, I suppose, the Nance family, lived on Tean in 1717. The island was uninhabited, regularly at least, when Heath was in Scilly in 1744, and when Borlase came over eight years later; though Borlase saw on it "some ruins and fields of Corn and Pasture." Woodley (1822) wrote that the house was still "occasionally occupied" and that the Nances living then on St. Martin's (where they have their descendants today) still held the island and cultivated "a few acres of it, leaving the rest to pasture sheep." The two granite mortars lying by the cottage may be of any age. Such mortars were used for pounding corn—used with a wooden mallet—as late as 1902 in Foula in the Shetlands. There are many of these mortars about Scilly; and many round querns, of the kind Heath found in use two hundred years ago. The islanders were still grinding with them into the nineteenth century, last of all for coffee beans out of wrecks.

Along West Porth the bowls of a kelp kiln or two are visible, and many more exist on either side of the ridge of Old Man. Much of the island, too, was walled off into fields, the lines of which are easily traced in winter, or early in the year. Before the Nances came to Tean, the island was briefly occupied by soldiers in 1651, in Admiral Blake's short campaign against the Royalist uprising in Scilly (see above, page 23. Scilly had surrendered to Parliament in 1646, but later the garrison had rebelled and gone over to the Royalist cause). One of the soldiers wrote a news pamphlet about these operations, in which he describes how they used Tean as an advanced base against Tresco: "We made fires upon Tean as if we had continued there, the smoke whereof was blown towards the enemy, which somewhat obscured our passage."

But what he called their "mariterrene service" was triumphant. "The Lord was our Helper, graciously answering to the Word given out amoung us which was *Help Lord*." They made their landing on Tresco, killed twelve or fourteen men and a captain, and took four captains and a hundred and sixty three other prisoners.

That was no more than an incidental interference from the larger world; and what I discovered by accident in one excursion to Tean was that the cottage of the kelping Nances occupied a very much older site as the true point of focus on the island. Between the stout protecting wall, which ran along from the cottage, and the edge of the sea there was a plot of grass two or three yards wide. There I noticed a dribble of limpet shells where the grass broke away to the granite of the shore. A little amateur investigation soon bit into the spill of a curiously muddled kitchen midden. Limpet shells, oyster shells, bits of the bones of oxen, sheep and pigs, some of them burnt, seal bones, rabbit bones, fish bones, and half of a well worn prehistoric saddle-quern used for making flour, were mixed with pottery and sand and oddments of granite. It was a mixture of the ages. Much of the pottery was mediaeval green glazed ware, fragments of waisted pitchers of the thirteenth and fourteenth centuries. Much of it also was scraps of a dark brown ware with markings which showed that the pots, when still wet and unfired, had been laid on mats of grass. Because pottery of this kind had been found in excavating a Viking house at Jarlshof in the Shetlands, I began to fancy there must have been a Viking settlement where the cottage stood, perhaps a raiders' encampment or temporary land base for raiding up the English Channel. But that was too romantic. Such grass-marked wares have been found since on many sites, in and out of Scilly, including sites around Cornwall. They date from the sixth to the tenth century A.D., so at least they gave a respectable antiquity—if not a Viking identity—to Tean's old nook of habitation.

But that wasn't the end. I always hoped something would turn up to link Tean with the British saint or holy man Theona, who gave it his name. Of this ghostly person I could find nothing but the late unreliable statement, in the *Iolo Manuscripts*, that he—decidedly he, not she—was a bishop who had been trained by the celebrated St. Illtud, and had crossed over to Brittany. Wouldn't he have founded an oratory on his island, since British monasteries or oratories were usually founded in person by the saint whose name they bore? The answer was yes. Professor Charles Thomas came in the nineteen-sixties to excavate the midden area and he uncovered the foundation of an oratory built about 700 A.D., of the same pattern as the oratory on St. Helen's. Underneath were a number of graves. Examination of the bones showed that some of them had been deformed by leprosy. It was as if Tean, in the era of its saint, had been a pest island, like St. Helen's more recently—a *leprosarium* of the Dark Ages, a place of refuge or exile for unfortunate lepers.

By a lucky chance, in 1933, another Iron Age find had been made on Tean, or at least on Old Man, into which the sea has been driving from the north-west, dividing it nearly into two and washing away the soil to the layer of "iron-cement." A cist, a small oval cist of granite stones, unworked, was noticed, excavated and photographed. It was presumably a burial. Among the finds were a scrap of bronze, a scrap of iron, part of an iron ring, limpet shells, fish bones, bits of carbonised oak and two bronze brooches. These safety-pin brooches were "among the latest examples of the La Tène style, and probably date from the Ist. century A.D." (*Antiquaries Journal*, July, 1934). Thus the human associations of Tean go back from the Nances and the Cromwellian soldiers through the Middle Ages and the age of the British saints to the Celtic immigrants of the La Tène cultures who pushed down through Cornwall and up north by sea to Scotland. And not many yards from this first-century cist (now all washed away) stands, or crouches, among fern and brambles the stone chamber on Old Man. From the cist to this megalithic structure and to a chamber tomb and a barrowed grave on Tean's Great Hill it is a jump backwards—back beyond the Celtic peoples, through the Bronze Age, across some 1500 years or more, to a culture between instruments of stone and the first instruments of metal.

So within these few acres of Tean there are evidences of the whole extent of the prehistory of Scilly. Old Man has its ancient ridge wall connected with the chamber tomb. Woodley thought he detected near Yellow Carn, the hill between East Porth and Tean Sound, "vestiges of a Druidic circle," i.e. the stone revetment which once surrounded a barrow. And Whitfield in *Scilly and its Legends* (1852) first noticed that from Tean there were "enclosures running far into the sea."

The Nance family hadn't themselves built the cottage on Tean. But they must have refurbished it. The parliamentary surveyors of Scilly had described the cottage as newly deserted and in ruins after the campaign of 1651. Astonishing it is to think of the long story of the site, of its intermittent occupation for something like 1200 or 1300 years; and it is, indeed, the one ideal spot on the island for shelter and for accessibility by sea. Looking back at the cottage from a boat out in East Porth, seeing it fit closely into the land, with a gorse-yellow hill rising beyond it, one can understand the affection in which this home must have been warmed. And Tean still keeps its benignity —at least when the wind is quiet, and the sea; it still seems humanised, still seems to invite settlement. But if there is fertile land enough for a flower farm, there is scarcely land enough for the two or three households which would provide a boat's crew and make such an extra-isolated life safe within reason.

The casual eye, the indifferent eye, may detect little enough in Tean. It may not notice that Tean is more than an isolated scrap of rock and land, that Tean is still richer in flowering plants than any other of the desert islands; its plants, the last living trace of the Nances, including several clovers and vetches, the common daisy, nettles, yarrow—and even the rare henbane. Yet Tean calls one to visit it again and again, more than most of the desert islands of Scilly.

In our own time no one has lived there for many days except the scientists, E. B. Ford, F.R.S., and W. H. Dowdeswell, who frequently camped there for several weeks at a stretch to investigate the population of Common Blues, by marking their wings with spots of cellulose paint. And they have experienced in their tent what storms can mean on the nudity of a Scilly island.

Anyone who wishes to learn more of this episode in the history of Tean and of genetics can read Dr. Ford's account in his *Butterflies* (1945) or the paper by Dowdeswell, Fisher and Ford on "The Quantitative Study of Populations in the Lepidoptera," in the *Annals of Eugenics,* Vol. 10, Part 2, 1940.

7
KELPING

WOODLEY HAS LEFT the liveliest description of kelp-burning, which deserves an interlude to itself after describing the island on which it was first practised in Scilly. "About three or four o'clock in the afternoon the kiln is usually lighted, which is done by placing a little ignited furze into the bottom of the pit and gently strewing some of the driest ore-weed on the flame, which by having the fuel continually renewed, in a short time becomes and remains a lofty and vivid blaze, surmounted by a column of snow-white smoke; which—sometimes ascending perpendicularly to the skies—at others, winding slowly around the dusky islands, and thence expanding in shadowy vapours over the deep, has a very peculiar effect, which is still further heightened by the number of kilns burning at the same time on the different islands—sometimes to the amount of forty or fifty." But, he added, that the smell made the islands offensive in the summer, clinging to everything that the smoke touched.

Kelp-burning is a poor man's industry, an industry of the Atlantic seaboards, West Cornwall and Scilly, in their less prosperous days, and more recently of the West of Ireland, the Shetlands and the Orkneys and the Hebrides. In Scilly kelping lasted about 150 years; and with fish, kelp was Scilly's chief export and a strong stay through a period of difficulty and poverty.

Kelp is the soda which melts out of the 'ore weed' or seaweed; and from Scilly it went by the ton to Gloucester, Bristol and London for making, chiefly, soap, alum, and glass. Woodley quotes an estimate that it took twenty-four tons of weed to produce a ton of kelp, by which one can guess the amount of family labour which went on all over the islands—cutting, transporting, drying, burning. The price the islanders got for their kelp in cash or in credit with the shopkeepers on St. Mary's was seldom above, and not infrequently below, £5 a ton. They needed little extra equipment, it is true; the weed was collected off the beaches and cut from the rocks at low water with a sickle. The heavy work was rowing and carrying the weed to the drying grounds; and what the islanders called "striking" the kiln, when the vitrified kelp was glowing and ready. Horse and carts, and donkeys even, are fairly recent in Scilly; they were, in general, an issue of that new prosperity which has led to the motor-boats and at last to old cars and rickety lorries on the off-islands. So, from the boat, the ore weed reached the drying grounds and the kilns by back and basket.

Kelping continued roughly from March to August, in the warm and sweaty months of the year. It was then that the Nances from St. Martin's would reoccupy their old house on Tean, and people, as Woodley recorded, would live for weeks at a time on Great Ganilly in the Eastern Islands in a temporary hut. No doubt kelping huts went up on other islands and islets as well, though Great Ganilly had a spring of fresh water. Extracts have been published from the 1787 Court proceedings of the old island Council of Twelve in St. Mary's (*Scillonian* No. 58, June, 1939), which show how jealously the islanders kept to their weed-cutting areas, just as the islanders kept, and keep, to their own fern splats on land. Two Tresco men, in May, proceeded against James Davies, his son, and Abraham Gibson "for going with their boat, cutting and carrying of the Ore weed from the Islands close to their shore which appears to be their property by Ancient Customs." The offenders had to pay 14 shillings for two boat loads, and court expenses of two shillings. Matthias Nance summoned three other St. Martin's men, two Woodcocks and an Ashford, for going to Tean, of which he was the land-holder, and "cutting and carrying of the Ore Weed to make Kelp." In the same month, July, Richard Ellis was fined nine shillings for taking a Tresco man's boat "from her Mooring to go to a different Island,"

and detaining the boat, "so long as lost him his Tydes Cutting Ore Weed to make Kelp."

As soon as one knows what to look for, it is easy to recognise the remains of a kiln, and to get over the belief that one has found some remnant of prehistory. The kilns were most commonly placed on sandy flats of turf, just above a good beach. All one sees is a shallow, round depression under grass or sea pink, about four and a half or five feet across. Jab a knife into the depression and it grates against the smooth granite bowl of the kiln. This is all usually that survives. The circular stone walls which were built up to three or four feet have been carried off for other uses, though on the White Island of St. Martin's there is a bowl still surrounded by the bottom layer of granite stones. Below Tinkler's Hill on St. Martin's one can also see the open bowl or base of a kiln cleared of its turf, brambles and sand.

8

SAMSON

FOR DECADES NOW SAMSON, most delightful of the hermitage islands, has been going back to itself. Its second depopulation, when Augustus Smith removed the inhabitants, was completed by 1853 or 1855. By the nineteen-thirties they gave up ferrying cattle and sheep to Samson for the grazing. Bracken reassumed its dominion. So really you should visit Samson in the spring before the year's new bracken covers up most of the traces of occupation, historic or prehistoric.

There were, according to accounts, ten houses on Samson; it is still possible to identify eight of them, all, except one (just above the sandy neck which joins, in the usual manner, the two hills of the island), on South Hill. A good many acres of South Hill, on the slope towards Tresco, away from the south-westerly gales, are enclosed with a high granite wall of regular, skilful workmanship, far superior to the modern walling that goes up on the islands. This, it seems, was built by Augustus Smith after the depopulation, since some of the houses have their front door opening out of the enclosure, and there is no gap in the wall on either side to let one into the fields behind. With its two gateways the wall must have been made to enclose the store cattle from Augustus Smith's farm on Tresco.

At least three houses were built on the high ground facing the Atlantic. Two more houses (including the one, from Sir Walter Besant's sentimental novel, known as "Armorel's Cottage") lie further down within the enclosure, side by side. Another house interrupts the wall at its northwestern corner. One, with its subsidiary buildings, is right outside, in a medley of old overgrown, granite-hedged fields, all fully open to the southwest. In April and May, when the bluebells are out among the young, sparse bracken and the figwort, all the field divisions, and the layout of the settlement are clear; and without much effort one can imagine the look of the island, peopled and under cultivation, imagine the houses with their thatch, or slate, and the smoke curling up—imagine, too, that as good crops could have been raised here, and could be raised here again, as anywhere else on the isles. The solid granite cottages are beginning at last to tumble. The unusual frosts of the winter of 1947 pulled most of "Armorel's Cottage" down to a pile of granite lumps. But the large cottage facing out from the big wall, at the top of the hill (though the roof had long gone) still resisted the force of the wind. The beam across the main fireplace still upheld its weight. The doorway opens south-west to the winds, and it is a fine thing to stand there and watch a big sea rolling in on a blue day, whitening Mincarlo and Minalto, and the other ledges and rocks a hundred feet below.

The vegetation on Samson is striving to become once more the natural community of a granitic island—bracken, brambles, bluebells, celandine (which must yellow its eastern slopes in early spring), honeysuckle, sorrel, bittersweet, foxgloves, birdsfoot trefoil, and the rest. But there are plants which still speak of an inhabited Samson—burdock daisies, a clover or two, privet, nettles, primroses; and the bluebells still remain thickest within the boundaries, on the eastern slopes of the island, of the old fields. The primroses, which I have not seen elsewhere on the Scillies except at one spot on Tresco and in the Old Churchyard on St. Mary's, grow in some quantity within the great wall; but on Samson none of the plants out of the Tresco Gardens have found a place for themselves. There are no trees except a large tamarisk and some elders which grow together among the ruins of "Armorel's Cottage." There is no mesembryanthemum; there is not a white flower of the early garlic, which is at once so troublesome and so pleasant on the cultivated islands.

It is this reversion (it seems complete when the bracken has died away into its full colour in September) combined with such obvious relics of habitation, which characterises Samson, deserted before the wind-break hedges, the flower trade, and the Covent Garden cheques so much altered the Isles of Scilly. So Besant's account of the affluence and comfort of Armorel's household is rather ridiculous fiction:

> "Opposite the fireplace stood a cabinet of carved oak, black with age, precious beyond price. Behind its glass windows one could see a collection of things at once strange and rare . . . . There were wonderful things in coral, white and red and pink; Venus's Fingers from the Philippines; fans from the Seychelles; stuffed birds of wondrous hue, daggers and knives, carven tomahawks, and many other wonders from the Fare East and fabulous Cathay. Beside the cabinet was a wooden desk, carved in mahogany with a date of 1545 . . . . No collector ever came here to gaze upon the treasures unspeakable of cups and saucers, plates and punchbowls. On the mantel shelf were brass candlesticks and silver candlesticks, side by side with 'ornaments' of china, pink and gold . . . ."

Earlier on, poverty on Samson was no doubt neither worse not better than poverty on the other islands, St. Mary's excepted, where there were additional means of a livelihood. In fact, from first to last inhabited Samson belonged to that limpet era of the Isles of Scilly which began with the chamber tombs and continued into the nineteenth century. Samson people may have had their small black cattle and their small island sheep, may have been smugglers, may have been kelp-burners, fishermen and pilots; but that limpets were decidedly a part of their diet, no doubt to the end, one may be sure from the three middens, two outside the three houses on the brow of South Hill, the other outside the cottage on the neck.

A little digging in these middens reveals a vastly greater quantity of limpet shells than animal bones, mixed up with early nineteenth-century earthenware of all kinds and black bottle fragments. The earthenware suggests that the Samson people had more coarse half-glazed bowls than fine plates and cups, less variety of household goods, in fact, than the Nances enjoyed in their seventeenth- and eighteenth-century cottage on Tean. There is not so very much difference, really, between these nineteenth-century middens on Samson and the two prehistoric middens on the neck of the island, on either side of the granite well. Both of them contain more limpets than anything else, both of them show four thousand years of continuity in diet. (One of the two prehistoric middens on Samson has yielded, among the limpets, bones of oxen, sheep, grey seal and birds, and bits of eggshell and black pottery.)

Woodley (who was one of the missionaries maintained in Scilly by the S.P.C.K.) records of the period around 1819 when the islands reached their lowest state in modern times, that the agent of the London Committee for the Relief of the Off Islands found in some huts "six or nine individuals crowded together indiscriminately on a most wretched substitute for a bed; having no other furniture than a large stone, with a sod on it, for a seat, and a couple of planks serving for a table." And one may remark that until a fairly recent date many of the Scillonian cottages were not built of granite at all. They were turf-built houses under thatch, of a kind which has not quite disappeared in the West of Ireland.

To give some dates to Samson, in 1651, as a result of the Royalist occupation of Scilly, the island was deserted and the houses were in ruins. In 1669 Count Magalotti recorded only one family, Heath again, in 1744, only one. Borlase in 1752 recorded two families. After that the population increased. In his book, published in 1822, Woodley wrote of finding 7 houses and 34 inhabitants; not much land was tilled, the islanders lived by kelping, fishing and a little piloting. Water was always a difficulty. Troutbeck's *Survey of the Scillies* (1796) indicates that Samson depended on the trickle out of the rock above Armorel's Cottage and the black brew from the natural pool called Southward Well. Troutbeck said the water became putrid in the summer. Both he and Woodley mention that the people went to fetch water from the other islands—from Tresco, in fact, and Bryher. Woodley in 1822 is the first to mention proper wells—two of them, on the neck, which were recently sunk, but "nearly choked with sand, the increase of which, even within the last half a century, is astonishing, and its destructive effect deplorable." His guide, a Tresco man, remembered that the neck had "consisted of fine meadows," forty or fifty years before; and Woodley himself found "a fine strong clay" some two feet under the sand. The last few inhabitants, still there in three or four houses, as the gradual evacuation went on, did manage to live in "comfort and sufficiency" (North's *Week in the Isles of Scilly,* 1850), if not with the chests of gold and precious stones imagined by Sir Walter Besant. Up to the end, the inhabitants of Samson were said always to have kept Christmas on the Old Series date of January 6th, sticking to the date because the Samson sheep, who knew nothing of changes in the calendar, still fell on their knees at midnight on the old Christmas Eve.

Clearly, Emperor Smith acted wisely in decreeing the evacuation of Samson instead of trying to resettle and improve the island. He was glad to have the grazing, no doubt, and glad of the chance of turning the rest of Samson into a deer park; but the population had gone up and down long before he took over in Scilly. Bad water, the frequent difficulty of the beach landings, since Samson possessed neither quay nor harbour, the absence of a church and a burial ground (the dead were taken over to Bryher), the drifting of the sand—everything was against Samson—except that Samson people liked their home and had no wish to leave.

It was on the neck, at the foot of the South Hill (in *Armorel of Lyonesse* Besant calls it "Holy Hill," as if it were still known by that name in the eighties—the "Armorel" farm was also called Holy Farm), that St. Samson's chapel once existed. The island is called "insulam Sancti Sampsonis" in the papal bull of 1193. If St. Samson had a small monastery here, the eighteenth-century meadows which Woodley recorded may originally have been the grain fields of the monks, like the fields below the monastery on St. Helen's. Without excavation it is impossible to find exactly where the chapel stood. The *Guide to the Isles of Scilly,* by J. C. and R. W. Tonkin (1882) places it at the foot of the north side of South Hill, and says that the remains were still visible, and that some of the stones "were removed at the time of the building of the Abbey House." Jessie Mothersole also mentions the ruins in her *Isles of Scilly* (1910) as though they could still be identified when she visited Samson. Wall foundations, whether of field wall or building, can be seen both east and west of the well on the neck, on slightly higher ground above the two early middens. Some of the eastward stones, in a hollow, are grown over with heather, and are not so easy to find. One could infer, Professor E. G. Bowen tells me, that St. Samson's monastery, or rather monastic cell, would have been founded on the island either by the saint himself or one of his immediate followers; and that St. Samson, while in Cornwall, "would have followed the favourite practice of the Celtic monks and retreated to the island for Lent or for meditation at other periods of the year."

On Samson one is inclined to speculate more on the people who lived in the cottages, on the removal of the last of them so much against their will by Emperor Smith, than on Samson's inhabitants in prehistory or even St. Samson and his monastery. Yet there is still much to be examined on both hills of the island. Three, possibly five chamber tombs in a row, near each other, exist just outside the big wall beyond the upper houses—one of them with three capstones in place and the passage underneath empty of plant or debris. But the summit of South Hill was rather too rocky and uneven for the grave-makers. One finds, on island after island, that they preferred the smoother downland summits, where finished, piled-up mounds showed more distinctly. So there are many more chamber tombs along the smoother heath-grown ridge of North Hill. The open tomb which faces Puffin Island—very easy to find at any season of the year—is crossed with one capstone, flat and large. It is one of the most dramatic of the Scillonian graves, and was excavated by O'Neill Hencken in 1932. Unfortunately it had been disturbed. Rabbits had mixed its contents up stratigraphically, though it was in this tomb that the excavator found the quern rubber laid in as part of the flooring, which tells one at least how the megalithic people of Scilly ground their corn. The barrows here—it happens again and again in Scilly—lie along the remnants of a wall, or line, of stones. There are such "walls," for example, on Northwethel, on Bryher, on Great Arthur, Annet, the Gugh, and Old Man. Nearby is the barrow opened by Augustus Smith in 1862, to reveal incompletely burnt human bones. There still is the neat rectangular granite box, with the granite lid tilted over. The two end slabs are fitted into grooves in the side pieces of granite. In all there are ten, if not eleven, barrows close together here on North Hill. At one time the passages were open in most of them, with the capstones *in situ*. But all except the two have now been damaged by man and weather.

From the grave opposite Puffin Island the ridge 'wall' goes off down the hill to the rocks at the northern end, towards an additional, unopened barrow. Two pieces of wall diverge at right angles as though there had been an enclosure; but the enclosure and these extra pieces are conceivably more recent, as if the old wall had been used for one barrier of a sheep pen.

An early wall of the same kind, a scrambled accumulation of large stones, runs on across the sunken land of Samson Flats. (It is marked on the two-inch Ordnance Survey.) O. G. S. Crawford (*Antiquity* 1927) has called it a field-wall, though, in fact, it appears as a single line moving towards Black Ledge, a natural pile of granite lumps which may have stood up considerably before the sinking of the land. The first to notice this submarine walling was Borlase, who saw, if his usually accurate observation was accurate on this occasion, much more of it than can be seen now—"many remains of Hedges ascending from the Hill (i.e., North Hill) and running many feet under the level of the Sea towards TRESCAW." He mentioned, though at secondhand, ruins which were revealed by shifting sands on the Flats; and also saw "Hedges of stone six feet under the common run of the Sand-banks" on the hill. Crawford was told of a similar wall running under high water mark between Samson and White Island. But in spite of Crawford and Borlase, it seems doubtful if the wall on Samson Flats was a field wall and not one of the walls which for some reason or other were made to link up the tenements of the dead.

Adding the evidence up, the early people of Samson must have gathered mainly by the neck of the present island, where the land, not necessarily the most fertile, would certainly have been the most sheltered from the prevailing winds. Though with windbreaks and pittosporum hedges much might still be made of the soil on South Hill, it is clear that Samson had long been a difficult island, clear that with shifting sands the decay in human vitality upon Samson had begun long before Augustus Smith took his decision to empty the island—however much for a little while the new population had increased between the times of Magalotti and Woodley.

9

BRYHER

BY ITS CONFIGURATION and its position Bryher has more variety than any of the islands. Low on the water, open to the Atlantic on the west, it is a series of small granite hills from Shipman Head Down to Watch Hill, Timmy's Hill, Gweal Hill, Samson Hill, joined by curved hollows which give the island an exquisite felicity. The felicity is strengthened perpetually by sharpness. The sandy shores opposite Tresco rise into broken rock under Shipman Head Down; and, between them, the rocks on the Bryher side of the channel as it narrows, and the rocks on the Tresco side below

Bryher

and above Cromwell's Castle—the best-placed building on the islands—form a savage gateway into the Atlantic; or rather, one of the gateways by which the Atlantic has driven, from a little west of north, into the interior of Scilly, into the old unified island.

The felicity, the intimacy, and the sharpness of Bryher are most admirably united in the scene from the Baptist Chapel westwards. Nothing is more surprisingly blended on Tresco, or on St. Martin's, or on Agnes. Left and right are the slopes of Timmy's Hill and Watch Hill, gorse-yellow in early spring. First the eye crosses slightly curving grass fields. Then the valley is filled with a medley of high-hedged dark-shaded bulb plots, the green hedges blown by the wind and breaking the rectangular forms with their untidiness. Beyond them are inlaid the close green flats around Great Pool; and slightly above, crouch, on the left, a few farmhouses. Gweal Hill and the island of Gweal rise on the seaward side of the flats, against the sea, a sea interrupted with a population of rocks. First, then, the tenderness of the valley slopes, the grass fields, the untidy bulb plots, the smooth sea turf around the Pool, and next the rock savagery—Merrick Island, Black Rocks (all of them look black), Castle Bryher, Illiswilgig, Seal Rock, Maiden Bower, beyond which the sun vanishes into the Atlantic.

In April, this valley is whitened in clumps and patches with *Allium triquetrum*, among the uncurling bracken and the dry brambles.

Turning left past the houses and along under Timmy's Hill, one walks over a wide sandy flat of sea turf, stretching along Great Porth, under Samson Hill, to the southern end of Bryher. The light of late afternoon and early evening strikes in across this western side, accentuating the seaward rocks with shadow, smoothing the smooth grass flats, picking out the houses in light and dark, enlivening the hill slopes.

Near the Pool, slightly apart from the other houses, which fit comfortably into the slope of Timmy's Hill, two houses in one stand rather uncomfortably across a neck of land, very near the shingles of Great Porth. One house is uninhabited, the other is a ruin; and the ruin is worth entering, since, like the ruins on Samson, or the seventeenth-century house on Tean, it shows nakedly the older building methods of Scilly. The house has two rooms up and two rooms down, massive granite walls, and a great rectangular granite chimney at the south-eastern end, built from floor-level to the roof. The partition between the two rooms, now falling to bits, is an island counterpart of the brick-nogging of the mainland, a framework of wooden rectangles, filled in with small granite lumps set in a light brown clay. Then wood and granite were plastered smooth with the same clay mixed up with a little straw.

This 'clay' is in fact the sandy 'iron-cement' above the still tougher matrix of Glacial Age in which the Scillonian flints occur. The geological memoir on the Isles of Scilly comments upon its use in buildings, and upon its property of setting like a cement. It contains silica and oxide of iron; the soluble silica becomes insoluble when it is dried, and silica and iron oxide together "evidently assist in causing this material to set when dry and bind it together with extraordinary tenacity." The deposit is what the islanders still call "rab," and what Robert Heath, in his *Natural and Historical Account of the Islands of Scilly* (1750), describing building methods, misnames "ram." The tradition of its use may be a very ancient one indeed. The bits of plaster in the monastery's building upon St. Helen's look like the same material. Borlase opened a grave on St. Mary's in 1752 and found mortar used in its rough masonry. Mortar was used (and is still visible) in the chamber tomb at Innisidgen on St. Mary's. When Augustus Smith carefully opened his barrow on Samson, he found "the bottom of the sarcophagus . . . neatly fitted with a pavement of flat irregularly-shaped stones, the joints being filled with clay mortar. The side stones were also cemented together, and the lid was neatly fixed with the same kind of plaster, showing that it had never been disturbed since its construction."

Now, the islands are becoming so severed from themselves and from their past that they are within the universal culture of concrete blocks and Portland cement. Concrete blocks, instead of the granite which lies about everywhere, make the new houses, or new packing sheds—preserving roughly the colour, but not the delicate tone of the older buildings. I have several times heard islanders complain that the old "rab" mortar answers better than any substitute. The earlier water tanks were built with granite and "rab," and leak less often than the new tanks of concrete block, sand, and cement.

The neighbourhood of the Pool has its other attractions. A decaying boathouse there shows the old method of Scillonian thatching, though the ropes with which the roof is pegged into the wall are no longer the old ropes woven of straw, and even a length of chain has been employed. Scillonian thatching resembles the thatching of houses on the exposed western coasts of Ireland—outwardly at least. First comes an underlayer of bracken, then rye straw or reeds from the island pools, then the criss-crossing ropes to lash the thatch down against the wind.

The pools are something one does not expect to find on Scilly. Tresco, St. Mary's, St. Martin's, Agnes and Bryher all have them, and all of them (see the *Geological Memoir*) are probably due to the deposit of iron cement which gives each pool a waterproof bed. The pool on Bryher, judging from the fact that it is called "The New Poole" in the Parliamentary Survey, has been recently formed (Woodley's evidence also suggests that the pool on Agnes is not very old). It has been formed, and is protected, by a bar of pebbles and sand lying between the pool and the sea. The pools now are more ornament than profit. They gave the islanders thatching reed, it is true. They gave the islanders drinking water—so, at least, the pool on Agnes was used—before the wells were sunk on the islands and before the Scillonians took to their modern habit of storing rainwater off the slates. The water looks scummy and unpleasant, but normally it is fresh enough, as one knows from an analysis of the water in the Tresco pools made by Sir Humphry Davy, when there were thoughts of enclosing the inland sea with breakwaters and making Scilly into a naval harbour. Woodley says that when spray or high tides made the Agnes pool too salty, it was drained by cutting a ditch through the bar into the sea, and then allowed to fill up again. Borlase found the Agnes people content with their bad water and too lazy to dig wells. It is no doubt on the damp, slightly brackish margin of the pools that the Scillonian mosquitoes breed— mosquitoes of the coastal *Aedes* group, which once caused havoc in Droitwich Spa when somehow or other they found their way inland to a salty canal. I have had some sharp bites on Tresco and St. Mary's in the autumn, but Scillonian

Bryher and the Northern Rocks

mosquitoes are not abundant enough to be a very serious or universal nuisance. One of them had to its credit saving a Tresco man from the effects of a bomb. He had been worried by the mosquito when the raid began and had drawn the bedclothes over his head. The bomb fell; and the ceiling fell all around the bed. But the old man, under sheets, blanket and coverlet, was neither scratched nor damaged.

Except for Troutbeck in 1796, every Scillonian author has ignored the mosquitoes most discreetly.

In books on Scilly, Bryher has always had the thinnest and briefest of sections and, in fact, one knows about Bryher less than about any of the 'big' islands—or several of the small ones—as though it had always been a secretive island in its own corner. There are few mediaeval documents which mention Bryher. It was not among the lands granted to Tavistock Abbey. It is not connected with any saint, Celtic or from the Roman calendar. It is the only one of the major islands, except Agnes and Annet, with an unsanctified name. Even Agnes has been changed into St. Agnes and possesses the dubious recollections of her St. Warna. Away on its own Bryher has kept its Cornish name. It was 'Braer' in 1319—and it has almost certainly the Cornish *bre,* hill, for its first element. "Possibly Cornish *bre yer* 'hill of the hens,' or *bre,* 'hill,' plus *-ar* suffix as Tamar, etc."

Like St. Mary's and like St. Martin's, Agnes was an island in lay ownership in the Middle Ages. Bryher, if it was worth owning, and not more or less wild, was perhaps not worth mentioning or arguing about. Perhaps it was desert. It was desert assuredly in 1579, when it was held by Christopher Coplestone, a Devonshire man who had acquired much property in Cornwall. It was well settled in 1651, though a century later Borlase records that "not many years since there were but two families in Bryher." Certainly most of the names of its rocks and inlets and features and

Boathouses on Bryher

township—Pool, the Town, Northward, and Southward, each gathered around its well—are English, and most feebly appropriate. Tresco and St. Martin's and Agnes have more Cornish names, St. Mary's has many more, in proportion. Everything speaks of an interrupted settlement and of neglect. Beyond the absence of a saint, there is no record of a church in Bryher before the one opened in 1742 and dedicated by Paul Hathaway, the Chaplain of the Isles, "to the pious Memory of all Saints"—a church since rebuilt and enlarged, and given a pleasant appearance of old age. Moreover, Bryher has never had a clergyman of its own, always borrowing the parson from Tresco.

Archaeologically as well Bryher has been neglected—even more than most of the islands. The eight chamber tombs and the great number of barrows, of which there are more than eight on the bareness of Shipman Head Down, have yielded up little or nothing. Whitfield's guide around Bryher told him he had once broken, while ploughing, into a barrow and "found there ten or a dozen pots of jars, full of a kind of gritty dust, exhaling a very fetid odour. The whole earth around was unctuous and black, and smelt unpleasantly. As soon as the atmosphere was admitted, the vessels mouldered away, and no relic of them was left." It was probably a late Bronze Age cemetery, the urns all filled with cremated ashes. Another urnfield (unless it was this one magnified through the years) was detected apparently on Samson Hill above Great Porth: "A huge number of pots apparently without barrows are said to have been destroyed."

The ups and downs, and ins and outs of Bryher, its quick changes of scene, and its altering coasts make it indeed a satisfying island and according to St. Mary's motor-boat men, it is the favourite of most of the visitors. "The Town," in its hollow under the clear green of Watch Hill, neat with its high-hedged, doubly protected plots, is one of the sunniest, most sheltered and coloured places in Scilly, concentrating, on a fair day, all the happiness of Scilly into itself. Even if a wild westerly gale is pushing and piling the Atlantic on to the Shipman Head rocks and the rocks of Hell Bay, and blowing the spray across the rocky neck to Smith's Hole, it will be quiet and still in The

Bryher Church

Town, and the water in New Grimsby Harbour will barely be freckled by the wind.

Woodley noted—and it is a good way of realising the ancient union of island with island—how New Grimsby harbour shelves rapidly up from deep water to the shallow, sandy flat between Bryher and Tresco. People who visit Scilly only in normal tide periods are not easily convinced by accounts of walking from one island to another. The low tide walk from Tresco to Bryher is easy enough (though a bit sharp on one's bare feet) several times a year. I have walked in the autumn from Tresco to Samson by way of Puffin Island and Samson Flats. And the walk from St. Mary's to St. Martin's, via Tresco, certainly has been made, if not very often:

> "The tides have been unusually low this week, which induced several persons to try a walking feat never in the remembrance of the oldest inhabitant performed before—namely, walking from St. Mary's to Tresco and from thence to St. Martin's. This was accomplished with only the inconvenience near the Crow Point of getting wet legs and feeling tired with a journey over a plain so long in comparison with anything we have on terra-firma."
>
> *Cornish Telegraph,* March 14, 1860.

Low tides, let alone extra low tides, give a new landscape to Scilly, give the islands a new foreground of wide, yellowish-white sand and speckled gravel, give new contrasts, new colours and combinations of colours, and a strange sensation of smoothness and ease. But I have had the experience within a single week of walking to Bryher and then being rowed across from Bryher to Tresco when a too brisk wind was driving the Atlantic in through New Grimsby Harbour. The crossing took forty minutes, and it was as much as the two Bryher oarsmen could manage. We crept out, or were tossed out from shelter behind Little Hangman Island; and I had to land quickly, and as best I could, on the rocks between Tresco Quay and Cromwell's Castle. It was a sharp reminder of insularity, and of the winter difficulties in Scilly, of the circumambience of the Atlantic, and the force of the Atlantic.

Thatched roof on Bryher

In spite of all such difficulties, Bryher possesses nothing more than a matchstick of a decayed granite quay just below the church. It is an island for beach landing, like Samson. And at the very low tides a boat has to make Bryher by putting in to the west of the island on the sands of Rushy Bay. They are in keeping, these landings and this lack of a pier and a harbour, with Bryher's secretiveness through history. Perhaps it is also in accord that Bryher, with St. Martin's, was the last island to preserve its sheep, which still ran on the Bryher hills only a few years before 1939.

10
ST. MARTIN'S AND WHITE ISLAND

ST. MARTIN'S again has been a secular island flanking the islands of the church, an island without a history; a curved ridge of sand-blown granite, long and high, less varied than Bryher, yet more varied in its scenery than a quick visit on a grey day would suggest. Perhaps of the big islands it is still the least known and (wrongly) the least admired. Its north-eastern shore, from St. Martin's Head and the white and red-banded day mark of the seventeenth century to its northern appendix of White Island, drops roughly and abruptly into the sea from a barren, more or less level stretch of downs. This rough coast is varied only by the long curved beach of St. Martin's Bay, from which the sand has blown up towards The Plains. It is the inhuman side of St. Martin's, open to the Atlantic, and uncultivated now or in the past. At one point on these cliffs great clumps of New Zealand Flax have naturalised themselves from roots shot down with household rubbish.

Cruthers Hill, St. Martin's

South and south-west of the downs the island slopes into valleys and hollows, into shallow bowls of land protected now and again by sand dunes. Here is the best soil for flowers, for early potatoes, for grass; and here on this side, facing inwards towards the lagoon, many of the houses and much of the population of St. Martin's have always been gathered. In the sixteenth century, the island, like Bryher, had lost its people. Even worse than Bryher, it had lost its old Cornish name. St. Martin's was then resettled with Cornish immigrants under the stewardship of the Godolphins; and it was one of these, described in the manuscripts as "Steven Treveleck, gentleman," who pleaded innocence for himself and his two boys in the matter of the pirates and the Frenchman's nuts and almonds. Most of the land went to waste when the Royalists held Scilly; and only two little holdings at Lower Town were farmed in 1651. Nevertheless, there are documents to show that St. Martin's or "Brechiek" was inhabited in the Middle Ages, no less than in early centuries, back, at least, to the megalithic period. And I have picked up sherds of green-glazed mediaeval pottery by Old Quay.

On St. Martin's the best chamber tomb is easily found on Cruther's Hill, between Old Quay and the New Quay of this century, where the launches put ashore their cargoes and passengers from St. Mary's. Troutbeck (1796) says that its cover was taken away for building houses, that there were two other barrows, one on each side of it, and a fourth grave, obviously a chamber tomb, "eight feet long and three feet over the widest part", across the bay near English Island Carn. Early, but not quite such early, evidences crop up from time to time along the south-western and southern shores, which slope gently up from the sea. In 1947, a winter fall of cliff below Knackyboy Carn revealed a long stone cist, empty save for two amber beads. According to Troutbeck many stone cists were revealed by high tides along the Neck of

St. Martin's overlooking Tean

the Pool, a few hundred yards to the west—as well as "human bones of all sizes." When the tides are low, along Higher Town Bay, fragments of ancient walls are visible and what may be a small menhir, or standing stone; and now and again the sand blows off and a small square cist briefly returns to light. I found one here in 1946, after a period of low tides and easterly winds; but the capstone had gone and anything the cist had contained had long ago been washed out.

At the eastern end of this beach below English Island Carn and the former chamber tomb described by Troutbeck, a huge kitchen midden was found a few years ago under the blown sand. In among closely compacted limpet shells, millions of them, were occasional fragments of pottery, and bones of a small breed of oxen.

The most pleasant places in St. Martin's are between Higher Town and the beach, and between Middle Town and Tean Sound at the other end of the island. The grey houses of Higher Town lie along the crest, between seventy and a hundred feet up. Plots, hedged chiefly with the grey-green pittosporum, slope down in close lines to the Green and the Pool. Beyond the Green are the sand dunes—with the rust-roofed boathouses at one end—beyond the dunes the beach and the sea. This bowl fills up with the sun, is sheltered from the north and from the west. It is an intimacy of defined order sloping on to the suavity of the Green. The road from New Quay and Higher Town past the grey box of the chapel, past St. Martin's Church, past the overgrown sand and clay pit (which gave materials for the early nineteenth-century houses of Higher Town)—goes across the Plains and then down over the hill to the Middle Town houses, and glasshouses. Level from Middle Town onwards, the road separates fields, granite and green-hedged fields, sloping up the hill one way, down the other towards the sea-line of dunes. A few Monterey pines, lichen-covered, and more than halfway towards dying, stand along the

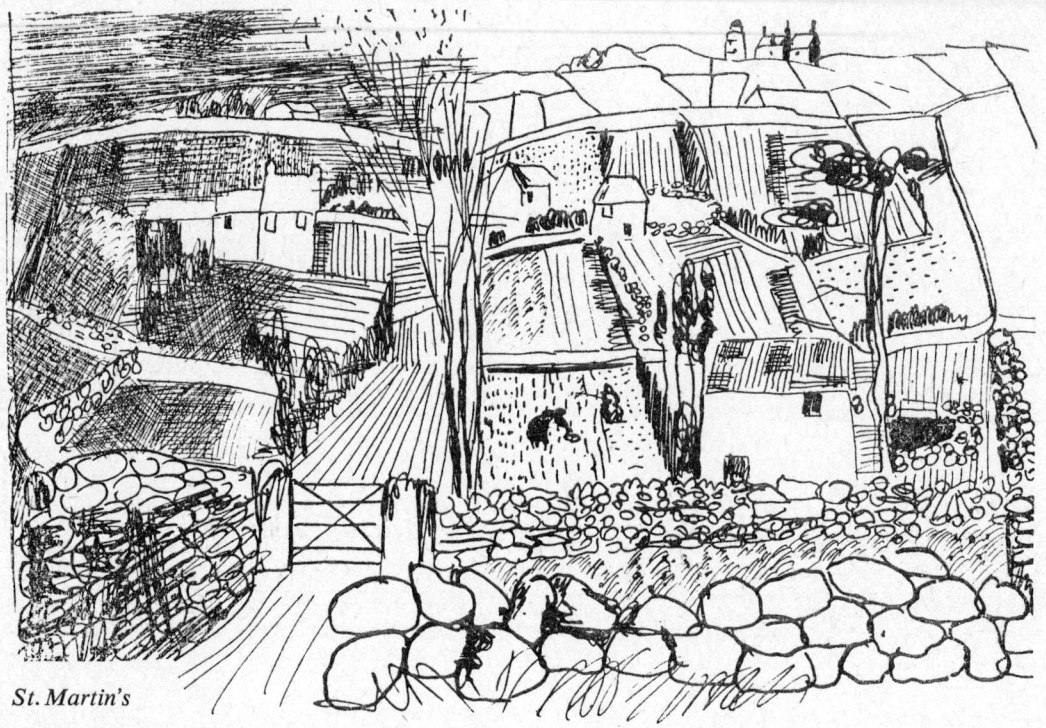

St. Martin's

road, and sing a bit mournfully in the wind. A few clumps of arum lilies, like large lords-and-ladies, push out of the brambles at the side, flowering in May or late in April; and in against the granite of the hedges grows a sulphur-flowered oxalis, which has spread to the island from Tresco across the water and has become a troubling and beautiful weed. Down below towards the sand dunes and along the Neck of the Pool, where Troutbeck's cists and bones were uncovered, are enclosures gentle as green cloth, with cows, and here and there a pale-brown young bull chained to a stake. Past Lower Town, the narrow soft road turns round the granite of Bab's Carn to the boathouses, to the yellow horned poppies, the seaholly, and the beach facing Tean, two or three hundred yards across the Sound. From here the motor-boats will splutter across the still water at the head of widening vee, taking the islanders on a Sunday morning across to the pale ale and whisky of the New Inn at Tresco, or, in the evenings, across to the cinema.

The evening sun levels itself against Lower Town and Middle Town and the fields and the pines, making the area one of an illuminated happiness. The sand dunes which fringe and protect this stretch of fertility are well matted and secured by marram grass and mesambryanthemum, introduced in the last century. On the seaward face of the dunes, above St. Martin's Flats, the patches of mesembryanthemum crawl up the sand, covered in May among the flesh of their leaves with large exotic flowers of a papery magenta.

St. Martin's seems to have been, and still is, an island little interfered with. For example, it lacks the old fortifications of St. Mary's or Tresco, or the lesser military works on Bryher, Agnes or the Gugh. Except for the seventeenth century Day Mark, and the ruins of a late eighteenth century signal station alongside, everything on the island concerns the island itself. Yet archaeologically it has suffered, if not so much as Tresco. It has its burial mounds, and the Cruther's Hill tomb, and

St. Martin's

the rocky chamber tomb at Knackyboy Carn itself. Between English Island Carn and Perpitch the protecting stones of a burial mound have been denuded of their soil (the Ordnance Map misleadingly marks them as "Stone Circle"). Old walling, as I have mentioned, is obvious between the tide marks at Higher Town Bay, about halfway along the beach. North of the island on the flat, just clear of the gorse, and just above Lower Town, stands the curious circle of stones known as the Look Out—there in Troutbeck's life and regarded by him as ancient. It might be (though probably it is not) the revetment, once more, of a barrow. Certainly on St. Martin's, on the high ground of the Plains and St. Martin's Head, much has been destroyed. Standing stones have been pulled down; ancient walls revealed among the gorse by a fire were broken up not so long ago. But every now and then some ancient oddment is newly revealed, such as the cist with its beads, or a crude urn in a natural hollow of the outcropping granite.

St. Martin's may or may not have been the mediaeval island of "St. Maudut"; but certainly it was the island called in the fourteenth century documents by the Cornish name of "Bechiek," "Brechiek," or "Brethyoke," an old name perhaps connected with the word "brych" or "breck," meaning variegated or speckled, an apt enough appellation for any of the islands. There is no record or sign of any early chapel or religious settlement on St. Martin's, which was outside the religious community of islands. But "Chapel Down," near St. Martin's Head, is suggestive. Early charts picture a building there which may have been a chapel, though it had disappeared by the time of the Admiralty Chart of 1792. But this chart, and most of the charts I have seen, from the Tudor chart in the British Museum, agree in picturing a church, or chapel-like building, near Middle Town, a good way to the north-west of the existing church. A hand-drawn Admiralty chart of about 1680, among the British Museum manuscripts, gives it a nave and tower. But all memory, and, so far as I know, all traces of it, have disappeared.

The modern church, inside and out, is the plainest of all the island churches—plainer than the Methodist chapel at Higher Town, to which panelling (white panelling, picked out in black and gold) gives a rough elegance. In the graves lie corpses washed up on St. Martin's between 1914 and 1918, named and unnamed, English and foreign. From another war—from Admiral Blake's assault upon Scilly—cannon-balls crop up now and then on the little rocky wart of Plumb Island, in the north-west of St. Martin's.

White Island (the White pronounced "wit") is hyphenated to the north end of St. Martin's by a shingle bar one can easily cross at low water. It is a long, curving island of turf, heather, bracken and bramble, with a rough eastern shore and a gentle sandy shore facing Porth Morran —along which one can detect several kelp pits. An old wall, now almost effaced, cuts across the neck of the island over a flat of big shingle and of sand. A piece of inexplicable walling, perhaps early or perhaps the remains of a sheep pen, abuts on to Porth Morran, a hundred yards or two further on. Shallow zig-zag and straight trenches here and there were dug out during the last war by troops on exercise. On the high ground, above the rocks on West Withan, stretches a ruined chamber tomb, about fourteen feet long, with one capstone remaining among the cushions of sea-pink and the brambles. Looking north, west, and east over the Atlantic, this was perhaps the choicest of the grave sites among all the islands, unless one might have preferred Round Island, nearby, where several barrows are reputed to have been destroyed in the building of the lighthouse. The West Withan rocks below the grave are nearly the northernmost point of Scilly; and since White Island is little frequented and lonely, these rocks are much used by seals. One can lie below the grave, and watch them, and listen to them moaning like children in pain. At high water porpoises in a shoal sometimes play around the calm lake of Porth Morran, racing, jumping and slapping the water. In May cuckoos take possession, fluttering and cuckooing as they go in circuits around the island, from rock perch to perch, or making long trips across the bay. Sometimes a black-backed gull lazily threatens the cuckoo in the mid-air. I have watched a cuckoo flying into the warm fog across Porth Morran, as though out to sea, until the bird became invisible and the "cuckoo-cuckoo, cuck-cuckoo" floated back quietly out of the grey.

The six-inch Ordnance Map marks "Aunt Elsie's Rock" a little to the north-west of White Island Bar. Near the rock is an outcrop of yellow clay which the St. Martin's people used for making their fireplaces.

11
THE EASTERN ISLANDS

WOODLEY SAW THE EASTERN ISLANDS as no one will ever see them again—with kelping in progress and "wreaths of smoke rising amidst the dun verdure and hoary carns of these petty isles," making them all the more, as they are indeed, "pleasing and picturesque."

They belong to St. Martin's parish, and have served the St. Martin's people mainly as a collection area for driftwood, as pasturage for sheep, and bases for kelp-burning. It is nearly certain that none of them have been regularly inhabited since they became islands. They have never been much valued, and so far as I know they are not named, one by another, in any existing document older in date than 1570. Even less is recorded of the Eastern Islands than of the death-delivering, ragged and black islets and rocks out towards the Bishop. Yet these are true islands, with beaches, with soil, and with the matted community of vegetation natural to Scilly. They are land rather than rock. Even the outermost of them, Great and Little Innisvouls and Menewethan, the nearest of the whole group to England, turn a green side inwards, however bare their seaward verges may be (Innisvouls is probably Cornish, *enes voel*, for "bare island").

These Eastern Islands have not been so agonised by wrecks as most parts and points of Scilly, though it was on Nornour, in July, 1872, that the "Earl of Arran" was lost. She was a paddle boat from Penzance with 100 excursionists on board. The captain had brought her close in to give the passengers (all were saved) a good view of the islands.

The most considerable, and the most worthy of exploration among the Eastern Islands are Great Ganilly and Arthur (always pronounced, as it should really be spelt, "Arter"). The two Ganinicks and Little Ganilly are featureless in themselves, however important to the eye in relation to their neighbours. This trio lack barrow or chamber tomb. Nornour, which faces smoothly to the inner sea and roughly to the noble Atlantic lump of Hanjague, has its own distinction, footings of a shrine of a Romano-British Venus, of the first century to the late fourth century. Among the offerings found by the excavators (*Archaeological Journal*, CXXIV, 1967) were little pipeclay Venuses, of a familiar kind imported from Gaul, little mass-produced nudities which derive in attitude from the great Aphrodite of Knidos carved by Praxiteles. Unexpected—and pleasant—to find foam-born Aphrodite out here in Scillonia. About Little Ganilly the most surprising thing is the long bud of the clearest sand, Ganilly Bar, which the tide uncovers, pointing inwards to Higher Town Bay on St. Martin's. Great Ganinick's distinction is the nurture among the scrub (find it if you can) of a single, three-foot oak tree—after a lapse of centuries the only wild oak in Scilly; though it was born perhaps of a bird-transported acorn from Tresco Gardens (J. E. Lousley, *Journal of Botany*, July, 1940).

One way or the other, if you visit the Eastern Islands from St. Martin's, you row around Little Ganilly over clear submarine gardens of chocolate seaweed, and land on the demi-lune of sand between Little and Middle Arthur. Arthur is one of the extraordinary islands. It is a trinity. Little Arthur links to Middle Arthur, and Middle Arthur to Great Arthur by shingle bars. Then the land rises to fifty feet high above Arthur Head. The trinity form an island of grass, bracken, bramble, heather, honeysuckle, sea-pink, and the rest, an island of scratchy, cushioned vegetation which hinders one's progress from Little Arthur up to Arthur Head. North (1850) noticed the ruins of two small houses where the kelp-makers had lodged. Whitfield (1852) though he could trace the "outline and materials of an antique pier." An ancient Scillonian told him he was right, that it was called "Arthur's Quay," and that, by tradition, "whenever one of its stones was by chance removed, some invisible hand always replaced it by night." "Arthur Quay" is how, no doubt more correctly, the name is given on the six-inch map, pointing into the western demi-lune of sand. I had not read Whitfield's book when I first went to Arthur and did not know that Arthur had had a reputation of making men uneasy; but certainly I felt it a curious place. The shape and physique of Arthur, especially at low water when shingle and rock and weed surround it and shut it in raggedly and disturbingly, deprive the island of the felicity of Tean, or the less emphatic happiness of Great Ganilly.

Knowledge of the barrows and graves on Arthur goes back to the scientific inquisition by Borlase. He found "three *Burrows* and the remains of Hedges, but nothing else remarkable."

Hencken lists five chamber tombs, two on Little Arthur, two on Middle Arthur, one on Great Arthur, but it is not easy to see more than two of them—one on Little Arthur and the one on Great Arthur—after the year's vegetation has thickened. One of the Middle Arthur graves is perhaps the smallest on the islands and the smallest megalithic grave known in Europe. The diameter of the cairn is $10\frac{1}{2}$ feet. The grave on Great Arthur is on the point nearest Ragged Island, and at a height from which the whole trinity, in fact the whole Eastern group, can be surveyed, as one sits on one of the three capstones, which are grey-blue and gold with lichen, and upholstered with sea-pink. I could find two pieces of ridge wall on Great Arthur, the one noticed by Hencken, which "has along it traces of little cairns or possible hut foundations"—"little cairns," i.e., worn-down barrows, seems more likely—and a further piece on the westward slope of the island. One of the chamber tombs was broken into during the eighteenth century by curious islanders, who found coarse "earthen pots" inside (Troutbeck)—probably it was the one on the high point of Great Arthur.

Any island, any islet, any rock that can be

landed on, is worth landing on; but as those who have written before about Scilly have discovered, Great, or Big, Ganilly is the only other one of the Eastern Islands that bears much description. It is a bold open island, built on the plan of Samson. In fact, it is a Samson in miniature with a smooth north hill, a sandy neck and a rocky hill to the south. As on Samson, the smooth north hill, rising to a little man-built cairn of rocks, 110 feet high, has its barrows. There is not much bracken on this heathery hill, and its south-western slopes below the barrows are broken by stumps of old walling which enclosed, at some time or another, rectangular fields.

Standing here in autumn, one looks down to one's boat drawn in on the new moon of sand in West Porth, below a curve of purple seaweed and a curve of green on the neck. Beyond, the bracken-rich slopes of the south hill, rising to a wild crest of granite. Beyond again, Little Innisvouls to the left, and Ragged Island to the right. It seems healthy, open, less secretive and more genial than Arthur. I think I have seen traces of the kelping hut which Woodley mentions on the south side of the neck, but I have not yet been able to search Great Ganilly early in the year. Where the spring was I do not know. Ganilly—("Goonehylly iland" in the Parliamentary Survey)—may be the Cornish *goon* + *heli*, "down," or "open land," + "brine"—the salt-down or sea-down. The meaning fits it very well.

One could make only wide guesses, or no guesses at all, at interpreting the names of most of the Eastern Islands. None of them, it seems clear, attracted the hermits of the sixth century and later. Only Great Ganilly had room enough for grain fields; and something, at some time, must have been grown within the Ganilly hedges. But the Eastern Islands have been, as they are still, little rabbit-run, neglected islets, neither fierce nor humanised. Picnic parties row to them from the farmhouses at Higher Town on St. Martin's, geologists visit them (Great Ganilly especially) for the clues they afford to the Scillonian granites and the formation of the whole Scillonian group. Cuckoos fly to them, hunting for victims' nests and for hairy caterpillars. Blue painted, brown-sailed French crab-boats, coming to Scilly (as the megalith builders, and the Iron Age Celts, including the Veneti, came there from across the Channel), shelter at night, from the easterly gales, in the lee of the Eastern Islands. Now and then a crabber gets driven ashore, as on Great Ganilly in the winter of 1946.

12

ST. AGNES AND THE GUGH

THE SAINT IN FRONT OF AGNES has no right to be there, and it is not usually there in island speech. It is a Norse name—almost certainly; the Old Norse, *Hagni's nes*, Hagni's headland.

Agnes—dropping the saint—is really the first of the Western Islands; most of which are small, flattish, and rocky-edged to a sharp degree, and inhospitable. The southern and western shores of Agnes have this Western Island character in a cruel tilted diversity of granite points and juttings, although the island itself around Middle Town and from Middle Town towards the church and the pool has a gentle enough construction. Agnes seems concentrated around its dumpy, white, seventeenth-century lighthouse, on the ridge of Middle Town, from which the land slopes placidly away to the church and the pool on the north and moves to a disturbance of rock southwards towards St. Warna's Cove. The quiet average of Scillonian architecture is interrupted here by the ugly house, too large for the scale of its neighbours and the scene, which has been built at the foot of the lighthouse, and by the gaunt row of costguard houses which seem transported to Agnes from a moorland mining village.

Agnes impressed Borlase as "a well cultivated little Island fruitful of *Corn* and *Grass*." Woodley declared seventy years later that its land was "the best cultivated, and consequently the most fertile, of any of the Islands." Indeed, the meadows, the bulb and potato plots, still impress one on a mild, sunny day with a sense of kindliness; and the island is open, without the hilly secretiveness of Bryher or St. Martin's. North of the main road, the fields are more uniformly hedged than on most of the islands with tamarisk, instead of escallonia, euonymus, veronica, or pittosporum. The lower, main limbs of the tamarisk writhe about on the ground, and the branches, seen in winter or in April, spring up and curve like a fountain blown over from the south-west. The bulb leaves between these division lines of wiry rust are livened in the early year by the magenta of the hybrid gladiolus, now naturalised on the islands, and difficult, one is thankful to say, to eradicate. Tamarisk was growing in Scilly as early as 1824, long before the other windbreak shrubs, but though it makes perhaps the most effective break, a hedge of tamarisk takes a great many years to mature, in contrast to the quick growth of pittosporum. Also, tamarisk has long been of use for making lobster pots; though most of the pots one sees now outside the farmhouses—even on Agnes—are willow pots brought over from Cornwall.

Bryher Church may look the one most in tone with an island, squat towered under its slope. Agnes Church, with its black, white and fawn panelling of the early nineteenth century, is the most elegant of the churches inside, and its position and the position of the churchyard just above the sea on a low platform, make up for its external shapelessness. This conjunction of rest and restlessness, of gravestones, church and Atlantic, reminds one of Lord de Tabley's poem, *The Churchyard by the Sands*, reminds one of

> Come hither, linnets tufted-red,
>   Drift by, O wailing tern

or of the verses in the poem

> O sea-wall mounded long and low,
>   Let iron bounds be thine;
> Nor let the salt wave overflow
>   That breast I held divine.
>
> Nor float its sea-weed to her hair,
>   Nor dim her eyes with sands:
> No fluted cockle burrow where
>   Sleep folds her patient hands.

The church is the second upon the same site, succeeding one built in 1685. The earlier church was probably not far away, but, according to Troutbeck, it had fallen into ruins, the stones were used for a house, and the house and most of the burial ground were washed off in a high tide in 1744. In Troutbeck's time people could remember an arch of "fine free stone," such as had been used in the priory church on Tresco.

Perhaps the earlier church had originally belonged to the shadowy St. Warna, the Celtic saint whose memory was still vigorously revered when Heath visited Scilly, the Agnes people invoking her as their benefactress and believing her instrumental in providing wrecks. St. Warna's Well on the edge of her cove is the only reputed holy well in the islands. If ever it had the kind of masonry one finds around such wells in Cornwall or in Brittany, all of it has long gone. Nothing is left but a damp and undistinguished little hole.

Just below the churchyard (in which one of the German victims of the s.s. "Schiller" lies under his lichened tombstone) bends the wild, stony, weedy beach and harbour of Periglis, into which an ugly high tide can roll out of Smith Sound. There was a lifeboat station here with a stone slip for high-tide launching, and a long wooden slip (now destroyed) for launching the boat when the rocks and the weeds were naked. It was a difficult, awkward, exposed place; but at least, before engined lifeboats, it was nearer to the Western Rocks and the ledges of the most mortality.

Every modern account of Agnes mentions the glass beads from some forgotten wreck which are found at Beady Pool, to the south-east of the island, across Wingletang Down. The places to look are among the rocks on either side of the sand. Broken bits are commoner than a whole bead; and—be warned—not one searcher in a hundred finds anything at all. Most of the beads of Agnes (some of them made into tie pins) were picked up, not among the rocks, but in ploughing the fields, into which they came with the seaweed carted through the centuries from Beady Pool. According to a report from the Ashmolean Museum at Oxford (*Scillonian*, No. 86, Midsummer, 1946) the beads were probably made in Bohemia or Vienna in the sixteenth century. Four kinds have been found, very small beads, faceted crystals, small dull red "barrels" sometimes striped with white, and dull red, narrow "catguts."

St. Agnes

The Scillonian also mentions "Crebawethan beads," reputed to come from a wreck on Crebawethan, out towards the Bishop. These beads are more elegant—barrel beads of a bright red striped with white, bright blue or deep blue faceted beads, about an inch and a quarter long, and "long cornelian-pink agate beads, faceted, about one and a half-inches long."

The dumpy lighthouse on Agnes is described at length in its earlier working by Borlase and Heath. It can hardly have been welcomed by the islanders, though it brought them occasional help in island affairs from the Corporation of Trinity House; and supplied them, before they sank wells, with much of their drinking water, collected off the lighthouse into a cistern. The Brethren of Trinity House finally obtained their patent for building the lighthouse in 1680, using to strengthen their request the loss on the rocks of Scilly that year of the "Phoenix," richly laden, from India. The coal-fire was first lit on October 30th, 1680, after merchants in Spain, Portugal, and the Mediterranean had been circularised and informed that the toll would be a halfpenny a ton on English ships and a penny a ton on foreign ships, either way. Collecting the tolls was not easy (C. R. B. Barrett, *The Trinity House,* 1893), and the Brethren had trouble, too, with their first keeper, who was accused of neglect and of stealing part of the cargo of a Virginian trader wrecked on the Western Rocks within two months of the lighting of the fire. He was a Cornishman; and Trinity House is said to have ordered that no other Cornishman was to be employed in the lighthouse.

The new building served until 1911, when the small modern light began to flash on Peninnis Head on St. Mary's.

The antiquities of Agnes, itself, excluding its neighbour and satellite the Gugh, have been neglected. Hencken, in the Archaeological Gazeteer, in his *Archaeology of Cornwall and Scilly,* mentions only a midden near Porth Conger (I have head of other limpet middens on the island, particularly on Troy Town farm). Later, in an article in the *Antiquaries' Journal* ("Notes on the Megalithic Monuments in the Isles of Scilly," January, 1933), he reported the low stone circle on Wingletang Down, where there certainly exist between thirty and forty barrows. But on Agnes the most fascinating antiquity—if it deserves that description—is surely the maze on the seaside turf of Castella Down. To reach it one takes the lane past the ugly block of coastguard's houses, which goes deliciously through fields bordered with windbreak shrubs and speckled with gladiolus, to the farmhouse of Troy Town. Below the farm a narrow gate lets one through on to the downs. The maze is two or three hundred yards along the coast beyond the rocks called, on the six-inch map, the Carns of Castella. There it lies, concentric circles of shore pebbles, half buried in turf and low heather. You enter between the narrow "walls" within which there is just room to walk, and wind your gradual way to the centre; then reverse, and wind your way out again.

In guide-books the maze is ascribed to the handiwork of some bored sailor in the eighteenth century. But it may well have been made rather earlier than that, the stones and sea pebbles having been renewed from time to time. It is this maze which has given its peculiar name to the farm alongside; the Romans played a maze game called *lusus Trojae,* the "game of Troy," so English mazes came to be known—rather late and no doubt through classically minded antiquaries of rectory and vicarage—as "Troys" or "Troy Towns". Common on village greens (and often referred to by Tudor and Jacobean poets), they afforded a simple kind of children's game. But these village mazes, of which several survive, were cut in turf. The Agnes maze or "Troy Town" seems unique in Britain, resembling in pattern and construction the stone mazes of Scandinavia (see W. H. Matthews, *Mazes and Labyrinths,* 1922), the first of which to be noticed in modern times, in 1838, was on the uninhabited island of Wier in the Gulf of Finland (others had been described by a Swedish antiquary as early as 1695). Many of these old stone mazes were recorded later from Norway, Sweden, Finland, and Iceland. Mostly they have a diameter of ten to fifteen yards—larger than the diameter of the Agnes Troy Town—and are found generally "on islands or close to the sea coast." The names they go by vary, but "more frequently they are known by some name akin to our 'Troy Town' such as *Trojin, Trojeburg, Trojenburg* or *Tröborg.*" A large stone maze at Visby, on the Baltic island of Gotland, has a design very close to that of the Agnes maze. Scillonian romanticism seduced me (in the first edition of this book) to supposing that this maze on Agnes, the island with an Old Norse name, near a spot called Gwavaberg or Garabeara which "conceivably contains Old Norse *berg,* 'hill'," went back to the Vikings.* No. But then the Scandinavian type has to be explained. Probably—and that would be interesting enough—the maze was laid out by sailors from a Baltic wreck.

From Agnes one can walk across, as the tide goes down, to the Gugh (?Cornish *an gew,* "the hollow"—a name suitable enough for the hollow between the large and small islands, much accentuated when the tide is out). The Gugh is coupled with two eccentric characters, the Mr. Cooper who leased it from the Duchy, not so many years back, built the farmhouse and buildings, died, and was buried, by his instructions, on Kittern Hill, the highest point of the island; and George Bonsor, who first carefully excavated a few of the Scillonian chamber tombs. One hears the macabre story of how Mr. Cooper was not buried quite deep enough. He was in danger, until he was more carefully tamped in with granite, of being exhumed by his own pigs.

George Bonsor was a wealthy Englishman living as an expatriate in a Spanish castle, much interested in Iberian archaeology. He visited the islands three times, in 1899, 1900, and in 1901, to discover, if possible, whether or no they were the Cassiterides, or tin islands of the ancients (they cannot have been, incidentally, though there are prospector's pits on the downs in the north of Tresco—probably of the late sixteenth century). Bonsor's excavations are described and illustrated in H. O'Neill Hencken's book and in the article I have mentioned in the *Antiquaries' Journal.* On the Gugh, he opened what he called "Obadiah's Barrow" (he had been shown it by Obadiah Hicks, one of the many Hickses of Agnes). Obadiah's

---

* *berg* or no, the first element of that name is Cornish, from the word for "winter" (information from Charles Thomas).

Barrow is easy enough to spot, a little to the north-west of the farmhouse and of the sand bar leading to Agnes, in among the gorse and brambles above Porth Conger. One can crawl down into the passage under the capstones. Bonsor discovered in it bones which "might have belonged to a skeleton buried in the contracted position with the knees drawn up to the chin," and above the bones broken pots, of which six had been placed upside down over human ashes—remains, no doubt, of a later use of the tomb. He found as well two bone points and a fragment of copper, or bronze. Long before Agnes people had opened a grave here on the Gugh, which contained urns with "ashes and cinders in them" (Troutbeck).

Hencken recorded, from Bonsor's notes, no less than eleven chamber tombs on the Gugh, of which seven have since been broken up. The Gugh has twelve other barrows and it has the standing stone, the menhir, known as Old Man, on the slope of Kittern Hill facing St. Mary's. The seven destroyed graves were aligned in a row along Kittern Hill. The Gugh, in fact, seems to have formed an even more crowded cemetery of the early dead than the North Hill of Samson.

South-west of the Gugh one can still see a piece, as I have mentioned, of the earlier fortification system of Scilly, an old gun-battery, or breastwork. On Agnes itself the sixteenth century piece of fortification which guarded the entry into Smith Sound can be traced still at the south-west end of Castella Down, not a long way from the Maze.

13
ANNET

ONE OF THE STRANGEST OF SCILLONIAN pleasures is to explore Annet (for which you will require permission, since it is now a bird sanctuary).

Landing demands a fairly quiet sea and usually means a quick jump and a quick climb up the rocks from the heave of the water running in Smith Sound. It is an island circled by rock and pebble rather than sand, though one can go ashore, if the tide is right, at a small sandy patch at the southern end. In size Annet is a little larger than Tean, but it lacks Tean's variety of height and feature and shelter.

May is the month for Annet. Its vegetation is less mixed and rich than on Samson, for example. But in May, the northern half of the island, beyond the usual neck, is a garden of sea pink, choking out almost every other plant except a sedge and *Sedum anglicum*. The sea pink cushions are two feet and more thick. Walking across to the heights of Annet resembles a bad dream of walking on huge sponges, without the rest which comes from intervening spaces of hard ground. In May, as the sea pink is beginning to flower, this sponge-garden exquisitely, at least, excites one's eye, however it tires the ankles. The sponges or cushions are outlined by shade. The unopened flowers are red, the flowers newly expanded a deep pink, the flowers some days' old, a faded pink or mauve; and the shadows of the flower-heads dance and dapple the cushions. Annet is too low and exposed for many of the usual Scillonian plants. No gorse, no foxgloves, only a little bracken, and here and there a patch of bluebells—the bracken and the bluebells on the southern half, which has more grass and less sea pink. From just above high-tide level, on the southern, lower half, an occasional colony of tree mallow stands up sturdily and unbent.

Tree mallow—particularly a plant of the uninhabited Western Isles, since it stands exposure, stands gale and spray—marks the major antiquity of Annet. On the west coast, facing out to Crebawethen and the Bishop, in the one sheltered spot of the island as it exists now (sheltered at least from the north, and the east, by a high, broken mass of granite), an assembly of mallow and the grey stems of old growth spreads over a large limpet midden. This Annet midden, white shells scattered over its surface, and only a yard or two from the sea at high tide, has been known for a long time, though, once again it has never been systematically examined. It does not take much probing to discover bones (I have had identified from it bones of oxen, sheep, wrasse, and birds) in among the endless shells, occasional bits of dark pottery, and (wherein it differs from many of the island middens) an abundance of flint fragments, many of them edged as scrapers. Just above the midden, eastward from the sheltering rocks of Carn Windlass, one of the odd ridge "walls" goes along for several yards, with what seems on its line to be remains of a chamber tomb. There is another such ridge "wall" near Carn Irish; and here at the north of the island there look to be several barrows.

Under its shelter of granite, grey and yellow with lichen, the midden site looks delightful on a good spring day, with the dark sea beyond, and sea pinks and bluebells in the foreground; but the spot has another character in a southerly or south-westerly gale. Borlase, again, noticed evidence of the drop in the Scillonian land mass when he came to Annet. He saw "some Rock-basons," i.e., bowls naturally weathered in the granite (though Borlase suffered from the Druid mania and believed them to have had some sacrificial use), "which, lying at present under full Sea-mark, are covered by the sea when the Tide is in." Also he reports that "the sand being washed away a few years since by some high Tides, discovered the walls of a house."

Rabbits live on Annet, as on most of the larger desert islands. As for birds, Annet has perhaps been made a sanctuary too late. Terns, puffins, the nocturnal Manx shearwater, and Mother Carey's Chicken still come there to breed, but not in the old immense numbers (though before they settle to breeding one will see plenty of terns, in their delicate white sharpness, turning and dropping into the blue inland sea). The greater black-backed gull also breeds upon Annet, as upon many more of the islands; and commits murder. Half-eaten shearwaters lie about among the sea pinks. But at least the gulls are being reduced by steady needling of their eggs. No one will ever have the ornithological pleasures upon Scilly of the nineteenth-century naturalists, who knew the islands before the existence of the motor-boat. No one will ever have the experience of Mr. L'Estrange in the eighteen-sixties, who sailed to Round Island through a sea "speckled with white," for miles upon either side, "by the silvery breasts of innumerable puffins." In his day Round Island was "the great resort and city of the sea birds." If Annet was another city, it was dwindled to a village. If one meets puffins still, it is in small parties and not by the mile.

The meaning of the name "Annet" is not certain. The earliest forms are the fourteenth-century "Anete" and "Anet in insula de Sullie." By the sixteenth century it was being written as "Agnet"; and in the Parliamentary Survey it is entered as "Agnet iland alias Annett"—as though (which the older forms do not support) the name meant "little Agnes."

14

ROSEVEAR

IF ANNET NEEDS A QUIETISH SEA, Rosevear, nearly two miles farther out, and a true Atlantic isle, needs for a landing a sea still quieter and flatter, and—preferably—low water. There is nothing between Rosevear and the open Atlantic but Retarrier Ledges, on which the s.s. "Schiller" so disastrously foundered in 1875, and the Bishop Rock. And this outward position suggests that Rosevear, and its neighbour Rosevean, are Cornish for "large headland" and "small headland", though a guess is no more than a guess, in the lack of earlier forms. As the motor-boat threads its way at low water round Hale Rock, south of Annet, round the pebbly island of Melledgan—which is not high enough above the sea for a growth of tree mallow—it meets stiff, rippling currents between rock and rock. One moves in a rock-and-weed-brown and sea-blue world which is distinct from the world of the larger islands and the central lagoon—a world beyond beaches, and beyond the ten-fathom line.

The route out from Agnes, from the difficult

Pereglis harbour, will probably—according to the state of the sea and tide—take one south of Melledgan and Greegan (mis-spelt Gorregan by the Ordnance Survey). The Greegan ledges, thirty to fifty feet above the water, will be tenanted, if it is nesting time, by gently grey, gently natured kittiwakes, whose presence is a sign of oceanity. Rosevear lies in the long line of islets and crags from Round Rock and Great Crebawethan to Pednathise—another of the sixteenth-century Cornish names in the Scillies. And Rosevear is the most westerly fragment of the islands on which human beings have ever lived. It was the nearest point to Bishop Rock—some two miles further out—where quarters and a blacksmith's shop could be established; and here, on this oceanic scrap, the workmen lived between 1847 and 1850 while the first cast-iron and wrought-iron Lighthouse—swept away in 1850—was being built on the Bishop, and again when the new granite lighthouse was going up, circle by circle.

If one lands on the south of Rosevear, one has first of all to scramble over granite, and then across an incline of sea-rounded lumps. In May, scores of razorbills will be grunting in the underrock crannies, or scrambling out from their single eggs and flying off to sea. Less expectedly a few puffins nest here in burrows under the stones. Then comes the plain, the flat, of Rosevear, a small green forest of tree mallow, out of which jut the fragmentary walls of Rosevear's peculiar settlement. It is a flat of an acre or two, with a shallow soil above the "rab." There would just be room enough to play cricket or to lay out a cramped football ground; but every part of the flat is spray-drenched in a high sea.

The boats, I suppose, were drawn up on to the granite-paved rectangle, bare among the mallows on the southern side of the flat. (It cannot have been used as a stoneyard, since the stones, shipped over from Cornwall, were dressed on Rat Island, out to which the pier stretches at Hugh Town.) Nearby is the blacksmith's shop, nearly gone, but identifiable by the clinkers still about on the ground. The building best preserved seems to have been the main barrack, a typical piece of island vernacular, with the windows opening out at an angle, giving the maximum of light with the minimum of window space. The foundation of one gable-end wall, and a good height of the wall itself, is formed of an immense piece of granite, outcropping from the soil. Little else is left except the stump of a flagpole and a granite platform on which there may have been a derrick or crane.

The engineer who superintended most of the work was James Douglass, afterwards Sir James Douglass, F.R.S., and his biography, written by Thomas Williams, says something of the "extreme discomfort and misery" of living on Rosevear. The men contrived to grow vegetables on the island, but when supplies gave out, and the relief had not arrived, they came down to eating limpets. The men, most of them from Cornwall, each dreaded the occasional chance of being alone on Rosevear; and felt that their ocean rock was haunted. One of the blacksmiths, forced to spend a day by himself as the only inhabitant, declared that he heard strains of mysterious music in the air. Their recreations included fishing and close acquaintanceship with the birds. James Douglass solaced himself with reading mathematics and engineering. But there was one evening—the sea must have been exceptionally calm—when the officers and men gave a "grand ball." The sheds were cleared, were brightly lit and decorated with bunting. The visitors came over in boats from Hugh Town. Dancing went on till the early hours in this most strangely situated of ballrooms, the guests departing in their several boats by a moon which lighted them through the rocks and ledges.

In May, Rosevear is thick with birds—birds self-confidently tame. The razorbills scramble out of the rocks and look at one before they fly off, the greater black-backed gulls survey one's proceedings from the walls or the boulders a few feet away, clamour round in the air, and swoop down towards one's head. Their nests lie about on the ground among the mallow stems. The shags are indifferent to a close approach. Round the houses lie rusted fragments of the hull of the "Cité de Verdun," a French mackerel-drifter which rather oddly went ashore on Rosevear in a slight snowstorm, when little sea was running. It was on a Sunday morning, in 1925, at a time when the islands were exceptionally and briefly snow-white. In one large fragment, divided by plates, the shags pile their nests as though in a block of flats. The birds own Rosevear, and few people ever disturb their possession. One of the Hickses of Agnes, an elderly farmer, told me he had been on Rosevear once in his life, when he sailed over to fetch a cut doorstep for a house he was building.

As for plants, I found four species, and no more—the mallows, growing even within the dwelling house, sea beet in shiny clumps, scurvy grass, and some orache seedlings. Otherwise nothing—not a blade of grass, not a tuft of seapink, though Rosevear can claim to be the host of fifteen kinds of spider, including one of the rarest of English species. The Bishop Lighthouse, the object of Rosevear's occupation, stands visible through an opening in the rocks from just beyond the houses, visible across the rough or slowly-swelling Atlantic.

Rosevear is well-placed in the wreck-yard of the Scillies. For a time, in its shallow soil, the eighteenth-century actress and singer, Ann Cargill, was buried, though later she was dug up and reinterred on St. Mary's. She was a short, thick creature, celebrated for her playing of Captain Macheath in a production of *The Beggar's Opera* in which the men were acted by women and the women by men. The East India packet, "Nancy," in which she was coming home from a professional tour in India, hit on the Gilstone and was then driven by the tide on to Rosevear, in February, 1784. All of her crew and all of her passengers were drowned. Ann Cargill's body was found, according to one account, floating in her shift, with a dead baby in her arms.

Fifty-seven years later, the steamer, "Thames," was lost on the Brow of the Ponds, alongside Rosevear. With passengers and a cargo of whisky and porter, the "Thames" was sailing from Dublin to London. A boat managed to take off the women. Then, as the tide rose, many of those who were left on the ship tried to make Rosevear, using part of the quarter-deck as a raft. The raft smashed up on the rocks. Woodley, in a pamphlet, described the escape of the one male survivor: "On the day after . . . although the weather was still nearly as violent as before, the boats again repaired to Rosevear to ascertain if anyone had escaped the complicated horrors of the preceding day." They landed on Rosevear. "But nothing was found except a few fragments of the wreck . . . and several dead bodies lying on or near the rocks. As the Islanders were about to return with these sad remains, they saw a man running towards them, and begging to be taken on board. . . . His name was Edward Kearons. . . . He was one of the steamer's crew, but had only joined her on the day when she left Dublin. . . . When the raft went ashore, he succeeded in climbing up a rock, where he sat for a long time, watching for the appearance of any of the men who had ventured with him; but in vain. Finding a cask of porter which had been thrown ashore, he stayed in one of the ends and refreshed himself by a draught. He then threw away the remainder and got the cask firmly fixed in a hollow place between two rocks; Where he partly filled it with some wild grass that was growing near the spot and slept there till the following day! (He was not above nineteen years of age.)"

Woodley adds a savage detail of this wreck, that "A few other bodies have since been seen, but not taken up, their mangled and mutilated condition rendering it impossible to secure them."

15

WRECKS

CALMLY PUT DOWN, and repeated again and again in books and articles upon Scilly, the statement that no rocks and islands have been more dangerous to shipping is accepted carelessly enough. But plot in the known wrecks on a map and the statement acquires life and horror. The trouble has been Scilly's position on the trade routes of the world. The shipping of the megalithic peoples, of the peoples of the Bronze Age and the Iron Age had to pass Scilly going north into the Irish Sea from Brittany and the French coast. From the Mediterranean, from the Indies (East and West), from the Americas, ships had to pass the islands to the great European ports of the North Sea, to the Irish ports and to Liverpool. Through two thousand or three thousand years the mortality must have been immense. As the sea routes run mainly south and south-west of the islands, as the winds prevail from south-west to north-west, and as the main multitude of the rocks and submarine ledges lie grouped to the south-west towards the Bishop, it is this area of the Western Islands, or Western Rocks, which has caused the most agony and disaster. They can be summed in that moment on board the "Schiller" at two o'clock in the morning of May 8th, 1875, when a big sea swept away the pavilion over the saloon in which all the women and children were collected. "Such a shriek as was raised I trust I shall never hear the like again," wrote one of the few men to survive.

In the time of sailing ships, Scilly, now perhaps less visited by the world's shipping than at any age in the last four thousand years, was both a danger to be avoided and a convenience to be desired. Ships crowded into the Road in bad weather, since Scilly united "the advantage of present safety with that of facility of egress when the wind shifts to any other point of the compass." So grew up the old profession of the Scillonian pilots with their long, narrow six-oared gigs. The haven of Scilly was valuable enough for Benjamin Tucker, afterwards secretary of the Admiralty, to bring out a survey showing how it could be improved, at a cost of £2,010,000, by building a curved breakwater in between Agnes and Samson, and a breakwater from the Gugh out to Spanish Ledges towards Peninnis Head.

The Scillonian (No. 32, December, 1932) published a list of the known wrecks from 1679 down to the last major loss—the wreck of the Italian steamship, "Isabo," on Scilly Rock, in 1927. Leaving out a number of ships which could doubtfully be classed as wrecks through the fault of Scilly, and several lost on the Seven Stones or the Wolf, outside the islands, and adding many which were overlooked, 526 ships were wrecked in those 248 years. Certainly a good many more should be added for the seventeenth and eighteenth centuries. The position of several of the wrecks is unknown. But the map will show that ships have been lost all around the archipelago; and of these at least 59 were lost beyond Annet, among the Western Rocks. 12 ships between 1782 and 1921 were caught by Crim Rocks alone.

Samson and Bryher and the rocks to the west of them have caught many, six of them on Scilly Rock between 1700 and 1927; St. Martin's and its neighbours, and rocks from Tean round to Ragged Islands, have had about 26. Agnes has had at least 20, and St. Mary's at least 30. Ships have sunk even within the interior sea, round The Hats, Crow Bar, Crow Rock and Guther's Island. To the known wrecks must be added all the unknown of all the centuries. Perhaps the monks of Tavistock had the dangers in mind when they gave their priory on Tresco into the keeping of St. Nicholas, the patron saint of sailors. They enjoyed, by royal grant, though with some reservations, all the produce of wrecks in the islands they controlled. Wrecks are specifically mentioned, as a likely source of profit, in later grants and documents dealing with Scilly. Sir Francis Godolphin, writing to the Lord Treasurer in 1577, had perhaps his special reasons for maintaining that "benefit of shipwrecks" was "not only uncertain, but almost not to be accounted" now that travellers were better acquainted with Scilly and better experienced in navigation. Wrecks had only been worth £20 during his captaincy on the islands, except, he added (and a very considerable exception), for about 100 marks of Spanish money.

Probably, there is not a fair-sized island in the outer ring on which the dead have not been washed ashore and buried. It was the earlier custom, not only of the islanders, but all around Great Britain, to bury the dead where the dead were found, as in 1707 Admiral Sir Clowdisley Shovell was buried for a while where he drifted to land at Porth Hellick; but in the last hundred years the five island graveyards have had their quota. There is a slightly grim note in the "Regulations in the Churchyards in the Isles of Scilly," agreed upon in 1914, and hung up in the Churches: "8. The Chaplain of the Isles" (now Vicar of St. Mary's—the title has been dropped, unfortunately) "maintains his ancient right to a fee of ten shillings on the interment of a non-parishioner, but in the event of a body being washed ashore this fee will generally be returned." It was in St. Mary's, around the Old Church, that most, though not all, of the bodies which came in from the "Schiller" were buried. More impressive than the big monument to the young and wealthy Mrs. Holzmaister is another of the "Schiller" memorials—the stone, on which the inscription will soon be illegible, to the 29-year-old Clara Just, "mit ihrem soehnchen Eduard"—her little son Edward, and her daughter Else. Mother and son lie together, but the daughter's body was either not recovered or not identified. "Ruh sanft mit deiner Kindern, du edles treues Weib, du gute liebrieche Mutter," the inscription says, "Rest gently with your children, noble, faithful wife, good, loving mother." The German, from the widower's instruction, was not very accurately transcribed by the monumental mason at Penzance.

It is not surprising that the Trinity Brethren gave themselves to drawing the teeth of Scilly, and began with the Agnes lighthouse in 1680—a lighthouse which itself caused the wreck of a ship, the collier which was bringing the coals for the old brazier, and which in 1764 hit on the raggedness of Burnt Island, just below.

Now, though the Corporation has lights on the Bishop, on Round Island, and St. Mary's, and has planted Scilly with buoys, it is rather beam devices than lights which have at last made Scilly less rich in disaster.

Recorded wrecks brought many mixed, useful items of cargo on to the beaches of Scilly, rum, brandy, wine, sugar, tea, mahogany, rice, fish, tobacco, wheat, pencils, table cloths, sewing machines, coal, oranges, Panama hats. When the s.s. "Sado" foundered on the Brow of the Ponds, in the Western Rocks, in 1870, she produced eggs, oranges, wool and wine. "The eggs were rather small, and although some of them were hatched, the breed of fowls proved unsatisfactory and eventually died out" (*Scillonian*, No. 11, 1927). This experimenting with hen's eggs from a wreck does suggest a similar origin for some of the species and varieties of Narcissus naturalised on the islands by the nineteenth century, with which the flower industry began. One, at least, the jonquil, *Narcissus odorus* (*Campernelle*) is known to be descended from two bulbs given to a Scillonian housewife by the Captain of a French ship. Others grew abundantly round the country house of the Governors on St. Mary's. They may have brought them over from the mainland. But it is not an extravagant temptation to think that they *may* (since the Governors cannot be accused of leaving behind many other traces of horticulture in Scilly), they *may* have washed ashore from one of the many Dutch wrecks. If one tries the experiment of putting wreck-eggs under a hen, it is as easy, indeed, easier to put a wreck-bulb into the ground. The story that the Benedictine monks planted the narcissi is simply a story. The last monk was out of Scilly long before any of the species or varieties had been introduced into England.

Some of the southern cultivation weeds, which are not natives of the English flora, and which go on growing in the friendly soil and climate of the islands, may also have come ashore in the grain cargoes which have descended so frequently upon the rocks. It would be natural to try sowing such grain, though I know of no record to strengthen the possibility.

Perhaps this is the point to include the broadsheet ballad of "The Rocks of Scilly":

> . . . Aloft, aloft, our Captain cries,
> Each man his post observe,
> And reef your sails before and aft,
> Our ship and lives to save.
>
> To the top went our boatswain's mate,
> To the main top so high,
> He looked around on every side,
> But could not land espy.
>
> Ahead of us a light he saw,
> Which did our spirits cheer,
> "Be of good courage, my hearts of gold,
> The harbour we are near."
>
> "About the ship," the boatswain cries,
> "And off the rocks keep clear,
> For on the deep we will remain,
> Until daylight does appear."
>
> "Sail on, sail on," our Captain cries,
> "We're right before the wind,
> For by the light we've seen aloft,
> We are not far from land."
>
> But as we sailed before the wind,
> And thought all dangers past,
> On the rocks of Scilly we poor souls
> That fatal night were cast.
>
> The first stroke our ship she got
> The Captain aloud did cry
> "The Lord have mercy on our souls
> For in the deep we die."
>
> Of eighty jolly sailors bold
> But four could reach the shore,
> Our gallant ship in pieces split
> And never was seen more.
>
> But when the news to Plymouth came
> Our noble ship was lost,
> This caused many sailors to fear
> The dangers of that coast. . .

16

MINCARLO, IN THE NORTHERN ROCKS

THE NORTHERN ROCKS westward of Bryher and Samson are more widely spaced than the Western Rocks towards the Bishop. They are most of them higher and more imposing; but they seem, since they are nearer to the two big islands, less oceanic. A few of them are, in fact, real islands, if a real island means the something added above bare rocks. Illiswilgig and Mincarlo, for instance, have their "rab," the hardness of which one needs only to test on one's hands and knees after a fall. Above the "rab" there is just enough soil to support, as on Rosevear, tree mallow and sea beet.

In character these rocky islets differ altogether from the small grass islands, the small grass scraps of the inner sea such as Green Island, or Puffin Island or the two Ganinicks, or, on the outer ring, the White Island off Samson and Gweal off Bryher. They are useless—useless and indifferent to human needs and aims. They have never grown enough to keep a single sheep from dying. They give you no welcome, and no one cares much for the trouble of putting an inquisitive human ashore on to their rock and weed.

Off Mincarlo, at low tide, its 300 yards of granite look huge, and black and formidable. Getting from boat to rock is either tricky in a normal sea or nearly impossible if the sea is too much on the move. It needs delicacy and skill in the handling of a punt. Achieving it at last, at the critical, still moment, leaves one to pick a way across a wide desert of weedy boulders. There is no level of soil, but a double hill of "rab" and soil which climbs up barely on the north-west side, and drops down on the sunny side through tree mallows; and the soil is only a little portion of Mincarlo's surface. One goes to Mincarlo either to see birds or to see how in hard cruel fact these outer defences of Scilly, on which so many lives have ended, are put together. Mincarlo's bird population is like that of Rosevear, consisting of greater black-headed gulls nesting among the mallows, of shags, of razorbills (and a few guillemots) and puffins, though I suspect most of the puffins one sees there are non-breeding. The Mincarlo birds, again, are little enough worried to be nearly indifferent to a man scrambling up the earth slope and peering about over the rocks. The puffins allow you to come within a few feet till you can watch the wind ruffling their plumage and blowing off a loose feather. Shag's nests lie about untidily, with a good many dry mallow stems in their pile of mixed materials. Blue eggs of guillemots, scrawled with black, suddenly light up a dark, rock-roofed passage, at the other end of which a single file of guillemots with a crested shag in among them are shuffling off to safety. The to-and-fro traffic of birds goes on past one's eyes. A puffin sways across to a rock five yards away, drops his orange legs, and lands. Four or five more join him, and contemplate you through red eyes in a neat, improbable face. A pair of razorbills couple on the next rock. This is not the secretive, protected life of Annet, among the sea pinks, where the terns scream overhead and the nocturnal shearwaters are visible only as corpses, as feathers and a dirty tangle of entrails; nor is it the island life of Bryher or St. Martin's with pleasure launches coming up to the pier and with cream teas and pittosporum hedges, dracoena leaves rattling in the wind and an echium in a warm angle of the walls. It is a rock life uninhibited and vigorous.

The only work of human hands on Mincarlo is a stone set up on its fifty-foot peak as a navigation mark.

17
ST. MARY'S

IT IS A PROBLEM, dealing with the capital island of the group. Large, as the islands go, flattish, and without a compactness of dramatic feature, St. Mary's strikes one as not enough, or rather too much, of an island, as resembling too nearly a dull chunk of mainland. Antiquities, fortifications, bulb fields, coves, corners, pools, marshes, downs, rocks, lanes, churches, eighteenth-century buildings, rare plants—St. Mary's has them all—with cars, a steam-roller, an air port, permanent waving, and hotels. There was a time when one could hire donkey-carts and drive off for a day's picnic in the "country"—in the interior; and St. Mary's alone possesses "country" and interior. St. Mary's alone is big enough for tarred roads, an abundance of cars and lorries and ugly housing, rawly placed upon its already plain surface. It has been always the secular island, the island of the ancient castle of Old Town, the island of the military governors, the garrison, the Royal Air Force, the Navy, and the agents of the Lord Proprietor or the Duchy of Cornwall. The blunt thumb of mainland authority has interfered for generations with St. Mary's, and now, in collusion with St. Mary's people, has very nearly succeeded in destroying its character.

The odd thing is how St. Mary's has smudged out the detail of its past—at least its historic past. Next to nothing is left of Ennor Castle ('Enor,' or 'Ennor,' was the ancient name of the island—a name of obscure meaning still in use through the fourteenth century, though by then competing with St. Mary). There is only a fragment of the Old Church, and in the fragment little beyond a few gravestones in the floor, and the Romanesque arch—the oldest piece of shaped ecclesiastical architecture in the islands. The church of Hugh Town (the settlement which grew up, to the diminution of Old Town, around the new sixteenth-century fortifications), has little of the interior dignity of its age, contains hardly anything of good craftsmanship except a coloured, gilded lion from the wrecked flagship of Sir Clowdisley Shovell. There were two early stone crosses on St. Mary's—they have vanished, though one survives in a photograph. If there was an ancient chapel at Holy Vale, the chapel has gone. True, Star Castle remains, with the fine gateway which leads into it; and some, at any rate, of St. Mary's prehistoric possessions remain, though perhaps scores of chamber tombs have been pulled to bits.

All these losses are the consequence of isolation, of having to make do with what was at hand and used no longer. Capstones from the chamber tombs were built into the pier at Hugh Town during the eighteenth century (*Scillonian* No. 30, 1932), and no doubt Ennor Castle and the Old Church were built into the better houses of Old Town. The new on St. Mary's has been a poor gain for the lost. There is a plain homogeneity, a plain decency of granite about the building of Hugh Town itself; but neither Augustus Smith nor his nephew who succeeded him, nor the Duchy of Cornwall, have shown much above a barbarian taste in architectural additions and replacements. Hugh Town owes its decency, first to Robert Adam, the military architect of Star Castle (though it is said that he used what was left of Ennor Castle in the work); a little, perhaps, to the military architects of the early eighteenth century, and more still to the unambitious, straightforward builders of the later eighteenth and early nineteenth centuries. A few seemly façades and doorways remain, but the good has been elbowed by solid monstrosity, on which the perpetrators have rashly left their solid initials.

The buildings of St. Mary's—not in Hugh Town alone—and their inappropriate siting, turn much of the island's plainness into ugliness, and a premature shabbiness. It is as much as sea and light and vegetation can do to keep St. Mary's as agreeable as one finds it to be after a while.

St. Mary's interior shores are tame, its oceanward shores broken and diversified. The island's most delicate scenery surrounds the semi-circle of Porth Hellick, a sea pool at high tide, backed by reeds and irises and a freshwater lake, and the gentle, willow-grown valley that rises to Holy Vale. Yet again and again, one is surprised into finding corners of the island more satisfying than one likes to confess. Fields edged with pittosporum suddenly give shape and grace to a plain slope. Suddenly one sees, in full sun, the pink-flowered length of an escallonia hedge, enters a watery lane, or emerges on to downs lit with sun and with gorse. St. Mary's after all, cannot evade its constitution, its speckling with island colours. And, as one walks around it, one finds the high points revealing deliciously the inland sea, deliciously exhibiting Agnes, the Western Rocks, and the two peaks of Samson in front of the evening light, deliciously sending one's eye across the blue levels of Crow Sound towards St. Helen's, Round Island, Tean and St. Martin's. It must be said for St. Mary's that it will always be the most select platform for revealing at a glance the happiest nature of the whole archipelago. When the light is dying away, the interior sea from St. Mary's resembles a lake ringed by pale blue mountains. And among the graves around the Old Church, in the sloping graveyard among dracoenas and unfamiliar trees and shrubs, one can feel as strong a dose as anywhere in Scilly of that melancholy which is not the most negligible attraction of the islands—native gravestones, gravestones of exiles stationed on the islands, of the wife of the governor under the Commonwealth, gravestones of the German-Americans from the "Schiller." There is much, in fact, when one is forced by weather to explore St. Mary's, to make up for the true insularity of such a desert island as Samson, with its ruins, or with the skeleton of a dolphin thrown by the Atlantic among the sand and the sea holly.

On Hencken's list there are eighteen chamber tombs for St. Mary's, of which four had recently been destroyed. The best to visit are those on Porth Hellick Down, where there are several (one of them the largest in Scilly), the grave on Halangy Down, abutting onto the wall of the last field before the gorse; and the darkly-opening grave at Innisidgen Carn, opposite the little island of Innisidgen. The large Porth Hellick grave and the one on Halangy Down were excavated by George Bonsor. He found pottery, and in the Halangy grave piles of cremated bones. Just beyond this grave, deep in gorse and brambles and hard to detect except in winter, are grouped the circular depressions of a village of round huts.

Since Hencken wrote his book, more has been discovered by excavation in Brittany of that species of cliff fort, of which the Giant's Castle, on the other side of St. Mary's, is example in miniature. The ramparts are worn down, and this fort of the Celtic Veneti has been interfered with by troops who dug themselves in nearby during the last war. Still, one can see how the headland was cut off and defended by parallels of rampart and ditch.

Coming back to the Scillonian capital, Hugh Town is an ancient dwelling-place—how ancient was first shown by a discovery in 1949 (*Archaeological Journal*, CXI, 1955). At the back of the town towards Porth Cressa, on the south side of the long sandy spit which is the "hugh" or hoo (as in Plymouth Hoe), workmen trenching for new houses came on two cists, two little granite chests. They had found a cemetery. Here, 25 feet above modern sea-level, excavation uncovered eight more of these little granite boxes, into which Scillonians had been fitted head to knees, with a few grave goods, especially bronze brooches of a provincial Roman kind. Then alongside was another of the Scillonian limpet middens. The little granite cists were made in the first century A.D., long, long after the time of the entrance-graves. The limpet shells had been thrown on the midden long, long after the cist burials—in fact, some nine hundred years later, judging by the presence among the shells of pieces of that grass-marked pottery which has come to light here and there in the archipelago. It took rather more than another nine hundred years to bring Scilly into the era of electronics and washing-machines, and helicopters from the mainland.

A long story for the modern inhabitants of Hugh Town to look back to. Thier midden folk were such as the hermits would have known, and such as Athelstan's men would have found on the islands. Among their limpet shells there was little in the way of fish bones, as if those Dark Age Scillonians weren't much given to risking themselves at sea, and there were only a few bones of oxen, sheep and horse. They were poor cultivators, poor herders and strandloopers, poor ancestors of the poor.

On Bryher, looking towards Tresco

BIBLIOGRAPHY

SINCE THE ISLANDS are apt to catch hold of visitors and make them return, here are lists of some of the books and scattered articles in which knowledge of the islands, their archaeology, their history and their natural history are best detailed and summarised.

Scillonian history and topography

(Benjamin Tucker).	THE REPORT OF THE SURVEYOR GENERAL OF THE DUCHY OF CORNWALL ... concerning the Formation of a Safe and Capacious Roadstead within the Islands of Scilly. 1810.
George Smith.	THE EXTREME MISERIES OF THE OFF ISLANDS. 1818.
	THE SCILLY ISLANDS AND THE FAMINE. 1828.
George Woodley.	A VIEW OF THE PRESENT STATE OF THE ISLANDS OF SCILLY. 1822.
	NARRATIVE OF THE LOSS OF THE STEAMER "THAMES" ON THE ROCKS OF SCILLY. 1841.
John Leland.	ITINERARY. circa 1540. ed. Toulmin Smith. 1906–10.
Jos. Lereck.	A TRUE ACCOMPT OF THE LATE REDUCEMENT OF THE ISLES OF SCILLY. 1651.
(Lorenzo Magalotti).	TRAVELS OF COSMO THE THIRD, GRAND DUKE OF TUSCANY. 1669. English translation. 1821.
Robert Heath.	A NATURAL AND HISTORICAL ACCOUNT OF THE ISLES OF SCILLY. 1750.
William Borlase.	OBSERVATIONS ON THE ANCIENT AND PRESENT STATE OF THE ISLANDS OF SCILLY. 1756.

John Troutbeck.	A SURVEY OF THE ANCIENT AND PRESENT STATE OF THE SCILLY ISLES. 1796.
William Worcestre.	ITINERIES. (1478). ed. J. H. Harvey. 1969.
Hitchens and Drew.	HISTORY OF CORNWALL. 1824.
(J. A. Paris).	A GUIDE TO THE MOUNT'S BAY AND THE LAND'S END. 1816 and 1824.
Augustus Smith.	THIRTEEN YEARS STEWARDSHIP OF THE ISLANDS OF SCILLY. 1848.
(Lady Sophia Tower).	SKETCHES IN THE ISLES OF SCILLY. 1849.
J. W. North.	A WEEK IN THE ISLES OF SCILLY. 1850.
H. J. Whitfield.	SCILLY AND ITS LEGENDS. 1852.
Walter White.	A LONDONER'S WALK TO THE LAND'S END, AND A TOUR TO THE SCILLY ISLANDS. 1855.
A. G. L'Estrange.	YACHTING ROUND THE WEST OF ENGLAND. 1865.
Alphonse Esquiros.	CORNWALL AND ITS COASTS. 1865.
L. H. Courtney.	A WEEK IN THE ISLES OF SCILLY, rewritten. 1867.
J. A. Froude.	ON THE USES OF A LANDED GENTRY (for Augustus Smith) in Short Studies on Great Subjects. 1877.
J. C. and R. W. Tonkin.	GUIDE TO THE ISLES OF SCILLY. 1882.
William Hardy.	BRITISH LIGHTHOUSES.
Thomas Williams.	LIFE OF SIR J. N. DOUGLASS, 1900 (for Rosevear and the Bishop).
S. Baring-Gould.	CORNISH CHARACTERS AND STRANGE EVENTS. Second Series. 1908 and 1925 (for Sir Clowdisley Shovell).
J. G. Uren.	SCILLY AND SCILLONIANS. 1907.
(various authors).	VICTORIA COUNTY HISTORY OF CORNWALL. Vol. 1. 1906 (especially Oppenheim's article on Maritime History).
Jessie Mothersole.	THE ISLES OF SCILLY. 1910.
A. and H. Gibson.	THE ISLES OF SCILLY. 1932.
Mary Coate.	CORNWALL IN THE GREAT CIVIL WAR AND THE INTERREGNUM, 1642–1660, 1933.
A. L. Rowse.	TUDOR CORNWALL. 1941.
Richard Crookshank.	ST. NICHOLAS, TRESCO, ALL SAINTS, BRYHER. n.d.
E. L. Bowley.	THE FORTUNATE ISLANDS. 1945.
A. K. Hamilton Jenkin.	CORNWALL AND ITS PEOPLE. 1945.
H. A. Lewis.	ST. MARTIN'S, ST. HELEN'S AND TEAN. 1946.
Geoffrey Grigson.	THE ISLES OF SCILLY AND OTHER POEMS. 1946.
N. Pevsner.	THE BUILDINGS OF ENGLAND: CORNWALL. 1951.
Charlotte Dorrien-Smith.	SHIPWRECKS ON THE ISLES OF SCILLY. 1953.
J. Dunbar.	THE LOST LAND: UNDERWATER EXPLORATION IN THE ISLES OF SCILLY. 1958.
B. H. St.J. O'Neil.	CASTLES AND CANNON. 1960.
G. F. Matthews.	THE ISLES OF SCILLY: A CONSTITUTIONAL HISTORY. 1960.
G. A. Gellicoe.	A LANDSCAPE CHARTER FOR THE ISLES OF SCILLY. 1965.
Clive Mumford.	PORTRAIT OF THE ISLES OF SCILLY. 1967.
R. H. C. Gillis.	THE PILOT GIGS OF CORNWALL AND THE ISLES OF SCILLY. Isles of Scilly Museum Publication No. 5. 1968.
J. H. Cooke.	THE SHIPWRECK OF SIR CLOUDESLEY SHOVELL ON THE SCILLY ISLANDS IN 1707. Isles of Scilly Museum Publication No. 6. 1968.
Elizabeth Inglis-Jones.	AUGUSTUS SMITH OF SCILLY. 1969.
Roland Morris.	ISLAND TREASURE. 1975. (On the search for Sir C. Shovell's flagship).
Michael Tangye.	SCILLY 1801–1821. 1970.
John Arlott, R. Cowan, F. Gibson.	ISLAND CAMERA: THE ISLES OF SCILLY IN THE PHOTOGRAPHS OF THE GIBSON FAMILY. 1972.
Richard Larn.	CORNISH SHIPWRECKS. 1973.
C. C. Vyvyan.	THE SCILLY ISLES. 1973.
Crispin Gill.	THE ISLES OF SCILLY. 1975.
A. J. Jenkins.	GIGS AND CUTTERS OF THE ISLES OF SCILLY. 1975.
Roland Morris.	SUNKEN TREASURE. 1975.

A quantity of information of many kinds is piled up in *The Scillonian,* the quarterly magazine of the islands, from No. 1, 1925. For Scillonian agriculture and the flower trade, see three articles in the Journal of the Royal Agriculture Society, 1870, 1890, and 1898. Also T. A. Dorrien-Smith, "The Progress of the Narcissus Culture in the Isles of Scilly," *Journal of the Royal Horticultural Society,* 1890.

Archaeology

Books, pamphlets and papers are extensively listed in Paul Ashbee's *Ancient Scilly* (1974), the latest and best book on everything from chamber tombs and flints and submergence to the Celtic Christian remains. B. H. St.J. O'Neil's *Ancient Monuments of the Isles of Scilly* (H.M. Stationery Office, latest edition 1969) covers with authority both ancient Scilly and the Tudor and Civil War fortifications. Read Ashbee and O'Neil, and you discover at once the great advance in the understanding of Scilly since the American archaeologist H. O'Neill Hencken published his pioneering *Archaeology of Cornwall and Scilly* in 1932. But his book is still one to read and treasure. Scillonian devotees should especially enjoy the following:

(tr. Morris and Magnússon).	THE HEIMSKRINGLA. Saga Library. 1891–5 (For Olaf Trygvasson in Scilly).
William Borlase.	"Of the Great Alterations which the Isles of Scilly have undergone since the Time of the Ancients." *Philosophical Transactions*, 1753.
S. M. Mayhew.	"Notes on the Scilly Isles." *Journal of the British Archaeological Associations*, XXXIII. 1877.
Glyn Daniel.	THE PREHISTORIC CHAMBER TOMBS OF ENGLAND AND WALES. 1950.
Paul Ashbee.	"Culture and Change in the Isles of Scilly," in Renfrew, THE EXPLANATION OF CULTURE CHANGE. 1973.
(Paul Ashbee, ed.).	"Prehistoric Habitation Sites on the Isles of Scilly", by Alec Gray. *Cornish Archaeology*, II, 1972.
D. Dudley.	"Excavations on Nornour in the Isles of Scilly," *Archaeological Journal*, CXXIV. 1967.
Sarnia Butcher.	NORNOUR. Isles of Scilly Museum Publications. No. 7. 1974.
E. G. Bowen.	"Travels of St. Samson of Dol," in ABERYSTWYTH STUDIES. 1933.
Helen O'Neil.	"Excavation of a Celtic Hermitage on St. Helen's Isles of Scilly, 1956–9." *Archaeological Journal*, CXXI. 1965.
Charles Thomas.	"Grass-marked Pottery in Cornwall," in STUDIES IN ANCIENT EUROPE, ed. J. M. Coles and D. D. A. Simpson. 1968.
Don Brothwell.	"The Palaeopathology of Early British Man." *Journal of the Royal Anthropological Institute*. 91. 1961. (For the lepers of Tean).
G. E. Doble.	ST. SAMSON. 1935.
	ST. MAWES. 1938.

Natural History

For plants the necessary book is J. E. Lousley's "Flora of the Isles of Scilly," 1971. Also it is worth looking up F. Townsend's "Contributions to a Flora of the Scilly Isles," in the *Journal of Botany*, 1864, written before the Abbey gardens had reached their prime and before the flower industry. Bishop Hunkin's "Tresco under Three Reigns" in the *Journal of the Royal Horticultural Society*, 1947, assembles much information about the introduced trees, plants and shrubs.

For Scillonian birds, E. H. Rodd's *Birds of Cornwall and the Scilly Islands*, 1880 and Hilda Quick, *Birds of the Scilly Isles*, 1964; the annual reports of the Cornwall Bird-watching and Preservation Society; for birds and other creatures C. J. King's *Wild Life in Scillonia*, 1942, The Isles of Scilly Museum published *Birds in the Isles of Scilly*, a handlist, in 1967.

For Scillonian beasts, including seals, dolphins, porpoises and the Scilly shrew, Edmund

Sandar's *Beast Book for the Pocket* is worth bringing to the islands. The Isles of Scilly Museum has also published a handlist, *Fish Around the Isles of Scilly* (1967).

See also *The Scillonian*, 159, 1964, for the anonymous "Some Memorialls Towards a Natural History of the Sylly Islands" (1695).

There are several special papers on the fauna of the Scillies, including W. S. Bristowe's "Spiders of the Scillies," and "Further Notes on the Spiders of the Scillies," in the *Proceedings of the Zoological Society*, 1929 and 1935, and K. G. Blair's "Beetles of the Scillies" (ib., 1931), and "Lepidoptera of the Scillies," in *The Entomologist*, 1925. The Scillonian sub-species of Meadow Brown butterfly is illustrated in E. B. Ford's *Butterflies*, 1945, and described by P. P. Graves in the Entomologist, 1930. But the amateur naturalist may often find himself foxed (though foxed is the wrong word for an archipelago which lacks foxes, badgers, moles, hedgehogs, and adders, and used to lack wasps) when he comes across some of the more eccentric occurrences of plants, insects, and creatures in and out of the water, from Portuguese Men-of-War to stranded turtles.

Geology

George Barrow. THE GEOLOGY OF THE ISLES OF SCILLY. 1906.
C. W. Osman. "THE GRANITES OF SCILLY," in the *Quarterly Journal of the Geological Society*, 1928.
J. A. Steers. THE COASTLINE OF ENGLAND AND WALES. 1946.
R. M. Barton. AN INTRODUCTION TO THE GEOLOGY OF CORNWALL. 1964.

Maps

The Ordnance Survey publish a special two-inch map; but even two inches to the mile is a small scale for efficient exploration of the islands. It is wiser to acquire the inexpensive six-inch sheets. Part of Scilly is covered by the 25-inch maps.

Worth having, too, is the Admiralty Chart of the Scillies (No. 34). obtainable from J. D. Potter, 145, Minories, E.C.3. See also "Scarcer Maps and Books of Scilly," Isles of Scilly Museum Publications No. 8. 1974.